WOLFGANG
PUCK

TOP CHEFS

OTHER TITLES IN THIS SERIES:

WOLFGANG PUCK

ALISON HART

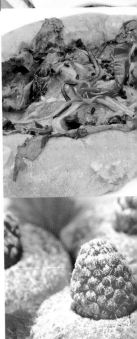

Produced by OTTN Publishing, Stockton, New Jersey

Eldorado Ink
PO Box 100097
Pittsburgh, PA 15233
www.eldoradoink.com

CPSIA compliance information: Batch#TC010112-5. For further
information, contact Eldorado Ink at info@eldoradoink.com.

First printing

1 3 5 7 9 8 6 4 2

Library of Congress Cataloging-in-Publication Data

Hart, Alison, 1950-
  Wolfgang Puck / Alison Hart.
     p. cm. — (Top chefs)
  Includes bibliographical references and index.
  ISBN 978-1-61900-019-3 (hc)
  ISBN 978-1-61900-020-9 (pb)
  ISBN 978-1-61900-021-6 (ebook)
  1. Puck, Wolfgang—Juvenile literature.
  2. Cooks—Austria—Biography—Juvenile literature.
  3. Celebrity chefs—Austria—Biography—Juvenile literature. I. Title.
  TX649.P8H37 2012
  641.5092—dc23
  [B]
                            2011044888

For information about custom editions, special sales, or
premiums, please contact our special sales department at
info@eldoradoink.com.

TABLE OF CONTENTS

Chef Wolfgang Puck holds a plate of Oscar-shaped chocolate statuettes during a party for the 83rd Annual Academy Awards event in February 2011. The Austrian-born chef has become a Hollywood celebrity thanks to his work preparing the menu for the post-Oscar ceremony Governor's Ball.

CHAPTER ONE

CELEBRITY CHEF

For the actors, directors, screenwriters, and technicians who make their living in the American film industry, no event is more anticipated than the Academy Awards. Movie buffs and celebrity watchers also look forward to the annual extravaganza.

On February 27, 2011, more than 70 million people across the United States tuned in to watch the telecast of the 83rd Academy Awards ceremonies. They were treated to a healthy serving of Hollywood-style glitz, glamour, and entertainment, seasoned with a pinch of controversy. Two attractive young stars, Anne Hathaway and James Franco, played the role of cohosts, bantering and flirting their way through the proceedings. Kirk Douglas—who'd attained the status of silver-screen legend years before Hathaway and Franco were even born—sparkled as a presenter. The ninety-four-year-old Douglas charmed the audience at Hollywood's Kodak Theatre while introducing the nominees for Best Supporting Actress. The winner in that category, Melissa Leo, left many audience members aghast when she let slip an expletive during her acceptance speech. The risk of more salty language seemed remote when Colin Firth was announced as the Best Actor winner. And, sure enough, the debonair Englishman—who'd portrayed a British monarch in *The King's Speech*—was gracious and droll in accepting his Oscar. Natalie Portman wasn't nearly as self-possessed when she won Best Actress honors for her work in *The Black Swan*. Clutching her gold statuette, Portman grew misty-eyed as she thanked her agent, her parents, her friends, her fiancée, and assorted others.

The show rolled on and on. Finally, after *The King's Speech* had garnered Best Picture honors, a fifth-grade choir took the stage and sang "Somewhere Over the Rainbow." With that, the 83rd Academy Awards ended.

Television viewers who'd tuned in from the beginning had seen three and a half hours of speeches, musical numbers, and movie clips—enough to sate the appetite of even the most avid of fans. On the East Coast it was past midnight, and a Monday morning rush hour loomed.

On the West Coast, however, the night was still young, and the movie industry luminaries in the Kodak Theatre showed no apparent anxiety about the approach of another workday. There was one more gala to attend. The headliner of this event, the Governors Ball, wasn't a movie star or a famous director or a big-time Hollywood producer. He wasn't, in fact, in the entertainment business. His field was food, but in that field Wolfgang Puck qualified as a bona fide celebrity.

CULINARY SUPERSTAR

As a chef, Wolfgang Puck has put an indelible stamp on American cuisine. As a restaurateur, he has redefined the way many people view casual dining and fine dining alike. Puck's ebullient personality makes him a natural for television, and he is familiar to tens of thousands of viewers of the Food Network and the Home Shopping Network, where he demonstrates his recipes and sells his own line of cookware and kitchen products.

Nowhere, however, is Puck more celebrated than in Hollywood. The biggest stars flock to his restaurants, and 2011 marked the seventeenth consecutive year Puck was tapped to cater the Governors Ball, the official after-party of the Academy Awards. It seems almost inconceivable that anyone else would be entrusted with the duty: for Hollywood's elite, Puck's inspired culinary creations have become as much a part of Oscar night as the red carpet and the breathless acceptance speech. To a large degree, in fact, it was Puck who made the Governors Ball the place for the stars to go after the Academy Awards.

The Governors Ball tradition dates to 1958. During its first years, the event attracted Hollywood's A-list celebrities.

CULINARY CORPS

Feeding 1,500 people—an average crowd for the Governors Ball—requires a small army. For the 2011 event, Wolfgang Puck had 350 chefs working more than forty ovens. The chefs, in turn, were aided by about 900 assistants and food preparers.

To facilitate prompt service of the food and beverages, the Grand Ballroom was divided into four sections, each overseen by a floor captain. Each captain was responsible for more than a hundred waiters, drink butlers, runners, and floaters.

Since 1995, Wolfgang Puck's Governor's Ball, held in the Kodak Theater in Los Angeles after the Academy Awards, has been the hottest party for the Hollywood elite.

In 1964, however, the legendary agent Irving "Swifty" Lazar began hosting his own Oscar night party. Lazar was one of the most powerful figures in the entertainment industry. He represented not only movie stars but also composers, singers, and even such major writers as Ernest Hemingway, Truman Capote, and Tennessee Williams. Soon Lazar's party had supplanted the Governors Ball as the preferred destination for Hollywood's movers and shakers after the Academy Awards ceremony.

In 1984 Lazar held his Oscar night bash at Spago, a Los Angeles restaurant Wolfgang Puck had opened two years earlier. Puck won rave reviews from the assembled glitterati. So perhaps it shouldn't have come as any surprise when, following Swifty Lazar's death in late 1993, officials at the Academy of Motion Picture Arts and Sciences—the organization responsible for the Academy Awards—turned to Puck to help revive the Governors Ball. The chef agreed to cater the 1995 affair, but he insisted on doing it his way. "The only thing I told them: you don't have no choice to what I cook," Puck later recalled. "I cook and you take care of the films."

Puck devised an eclectic menu. Hors d'oeuvres included roasted potatoes and caviar, vegetable spring rolls, and a variety of pizzas. For appetizers, Puck served salmon on Oscar-shaped crackers, seared tuna, shrimp, and asparagus. Roasted salmon and lamb chops were the entrees, and for dessert guests enjoyed a chocolate coffee cake with fresh berries.

Wolfgang Puck has cooked for every U.S. president from Gerald Ford to Barack Obama.

The 1995 Governors Ball was pronounced a rousing success. The Academy of Motion Picture Arts and Sciences asked Puck to cater the event again in 1996. Not coincidentally, perhaps, the Governors Ball quickly got back its mojo, becoming once again the consensus choice as Hollywood's hottest post-Oscar party. Puck has been in charge of the menu ever since.

ALL ABOUT THE FOOD

For Wolfgang Puck, a successful Governors Ball—like any memorable dining experience—begins with excellent food. "The celebrities who come to the Oscars ceremony haven't eaten for hours," Puck noted, "so when they come to our dinner, they're hungry and they expect great food."

Even for a culinary talent like Puck, meeting those expectations can be a challenge. For starters, the Academy Awards ceremony is notorious for not finishing on schedule, but the 1,500-plus guests who attend the Governors Ball wouldn't want to be kept waiting for their food. One way Puck makes sure this doesn't happen is by choosing dishes that aren't too complicated to prepare. "Don't look for Oscar night to ever feature chocolate soufflés," he told the magazine *Variety*, "because we couldn't fix them fast enough."

Even with judicious selection of the menu, good timing is essential to ensure that the food is fresh and flavorful yet served at the correct temperature. For example, hot entrees must go into the ovens before the guests arrive—but if the food goes in too soon it might be overdone (or lukewarm) by the time the guests sit down to eat. At a recent Governors Ball, Puck—who's in charge of hundreds of chefs and assistants during the event—ordered the salads prepared when the Oscar for Best Actor was announced. The presentation of

Wolfgang looks over the food his staff is preparing for the Governor's Ball, including a tray of Oscar-shaped salmon pizzas and a plate of black and white truffles.

the Academy Award for Best Picture was the cue to begin the main course. Desserts weren't arranged on the plates and the twenty-four-foot chocolate buffet table until the crowd exited the Kodak Theatre. (The Grand Ballroom, where the Governors Ball takes place, is located in the same entertainment complex that houses the Kodak Theatre.)

Over the years, Puck and his team have mastered the logistics of catering large events. But while great service may be necessary to please the demanding crowd at the Governors Ball, it certainly isn't sufficient. What delights the stars, year after year, is the cooking. Puck's dishes are invariably delectable and imaginative.

Every year the Governors Ball has a theme, and Puck devises his menu to fit. The 2011 ball had a Copacabana theme, so Puck worked Latin flavors into his dishes. His asparagus salad, for example, contained Iberico ham from Spain, along with black truffle aioli and mizuna leaves. Puck also offered his take on the classic Spanish dish paella. His Black Swan paella—named in honor of the Academy Award–nominated film—featured vegetables, saffron, white wine, chili, and parsley. Puck also gave a culinary shout-out to Best Picture winner *The King's Speech* with a typical British

Wolfgang's culinary creations for the Governors Ball are so popular they are previewed on the Academy Awards show's red carpet.

The 2011 Governors Ball featured plenty of seafood, including 1,800 pounds of Dover sole, 1,200 oysters, 1,000 spiny lobsters, 500 pounds of smoked salmon, and 40 pounds of caviar.

dish, Dover sole. Yet Puck's Dover sole was anything but typical: he pan-roasted it with fennel, olives, haricots verts, tomatoes, lemon, sherry, and olive oil. The 2011 Governors Ball guests were also treated to a black truffle pizza with ricotta and thyme.

As usual, Puck was a whirl of activity during the 2011 Governors Ball. He chopped and grated, just like the more than three hundred chefs working under him. He obsessively sampled the dishes to make sure everything was perfect. "I taste and taste and taste," Puck once said about the secret to his success, "but I never sit down." Because he treats the Governors Ball as if it were a party he personally is hosting, Puck also tried to greet all the guests, from the superstar actors and blockbuster directors to the sound technicians.

For the final touch of the evening, every guest at the 2011 Governors Ball received an edible Oscar statuette. It was made of chocolate—chocolate airbrushed with 24-karat gold. The confection didn't seem inappropriate in Hollywood, a place known for outsized dreams. Wolfgang Puck knows a bit about that subject.

CHAPTER TWO

EARLY INFLUENCES

Though he would pioneer a style of cooking known as California cuisine, Wolfgang Puck began life far from the bustling cities and sun-drenched beaches of the Golden State. He spent his first eighteen years in the Alps of Austria.

The future celebrity chef was born Wolfgang Johannes Topfschnig on July 8, 1949, in St. Veit, Austria. His unmarried mother, Maria Worth, was left to raise the child on her own when her partner, a butcher, abandoned her before Wolfgang's birth.

When Wolfgang was six years old, his mother married Josef Puck, a coal miner and former boxing champion. Soon after the wedding, he agreed to adopt the boy.

The Pucks weren't wealthy by any stretch of the imagination. The family home, a chalet nestled on a hillside, had no running water and no indoor plumbing. Because he worked in mines throughout Austria, Josef Puck was absent for long periods. During summers, Maria Puck also worked a significant distance from home. She was a pastry chef at the Hotel

Wolfgang Puck grew up in the mountain village of St. Veit, which is located on the Glan River in southern Austria. Today the village has a population of about 12,700.

Linde in Wörther See, about twenty miles away from St. Veit. As a result, Wolfgang and his siblings—who eventually came to include younger sisters Christine and Maria and younger brother Klaus—were often in the care of their grandmother.

A Chef's Childhood

Wolfgang grew up inspired and encouraged by his mother. "His mother is an exquisite cook," recalled Mickey Kanolzer, an executive at one of Puck's restaurant enterprises who also grew up in St. Veit. "I think his talent is definitely coming from her and was nurtured by her." During the week, Maria

A LAND OF CULINARY ATTRACTIONS

Austria, Wolfgang Puck's native land, is a prime destination for travelers who love fine food and unique restaurant experiences. Among other attractions, the country boasts an establishment believed to be the world's oldest continuously operating restaurant and inn. Located inside the walls of a monastery in Salzburg, Stiftskeller St. Peter has been in business since at least A.D. 803. Charlemagne, the king of the Franks and founder of the Holy Roman Empire, is said to have dined at Stiftskeller St. Peter.

Puck would make creamy mashed potatoes and soup from the fresh, ripe vegetables in her garden.

Puck's grandmother also influenced his culinary development. On Sundays, her beef bouillon would simmer on the stove. She also made traditional Austrian dishes like Spaetzle (handmade egg-and-flour dumplings), Tafelspitz (Viennese boiled beef), Rindsgulasch (beef goulash), and Kasenudeln (a ravioli made with curd cheese and mint).

"I have loved food as a very young boy," the chef would write in his autobiography, *Wolfgang Puck: Adventures in the Kitchen*. "The smells of the kitchen are as aromatic to me as the finest perfume."

If Puck loved food from an early age, he also demonstrated an unusual gift. His sense of taste was, and is, extremely acute. "I'm still in awe of his ability to dissect any dish he tastes," Kanolzer noted. "He can tell you every ingredient in a dish, and he is unmatched in that regard. Obviously, that is why he is who he is."

Since his childhood years, Puck has particularly enjoyed sweets. "Dessert," he once wrote, "has always been the highlight of the meal for me, perhaps because my mother was a great baker and I grew up surrounded by delicious pastries." During the Christmas season, Maria Puck made vanilla crescents and meringues. Her son's favorites, however, were her Linzer Tortes, a specialty originating from the Austrian city of Linz. Roasted hazelnuts, raspberry jam, orange zest, and cinnamon combined to create a delicious, lattice-top pastry. His mother also made Sacher Torte (chocolate cake) and Reindling, a yeast cake with cinnamon and raisins.

At ten years of age, Wolfgang Puck tried his own hand at baking. He made his mom a marble cake for Mother's Day.

A DIFFICULT RELATIONSHIP

If Wolfgang Puck enjoyed a close relationship with his mother, he and his stepfather often clashed. Josef Puck was a stern

A slice of Linzer Torte, one of Wolfgang's favorite desserts when he was a child. This pastry, with its traditional lattice of dough strips, is usually eaten at Christmas and other holidays. The earliest known recipe for Linzer Torte dates from the 1650s, making it one of the oldest recipes in the world.

disciplinarian who demanded obedience. He also expected his children to excel in school. "I never had fun on my birthday," the chef later recalled. "It's in July, and that was around the time we had exams. Father would say, 'Go into the forest and pick a stick for me to beat you with.' "

Josef Puck also had old-fashioned views about masculinity. The former boxing champ thought his stepson should take an interest in the ring. "He wanted me to fight," Wolfgang Puck remembered, "but I didn't like people hitting me on the nose."

As a young teenager, Wolfgang dreamed of becoming an architect. But the Puck family didn't have the money to put him through architecture school, so he instead decided on a career as a chef. His stepfather was aghast. "Our father worked the mines," Wolfgang's sister Christine recalled. "He said a man should work—men should not be in the kitchen."

During summers, Wolfgang sometimes visited his mother at the Hotel Linde, and the staff there got to know him. The hotel's manager, knowing that the youth was interested in a career as a chef, recommended Wolfgang for a chef's apprenticeship at the Hotel Post in Villach, Austria.

Wolfgang decided to give it a try, even though his stepfather strenuously objected. "My father told me, 'You are a good for nothing, you will come back in three weeks and I said 'I am never coming home,'" Puck told CNN. "I said, 'One day I'm going to come in my Mercedes and drive through your house—you will see!'"

At age fourteen, Wolfgang Puck boarded a train as his mother and grandmother waved goodbye. About fifty miles down the line lay Villach.

THE EDUCATION OF A CHEF

The Hotel Post is a charming structure that dates to the early

1500s. Wolfgang Puck would have few pleasant memories of the historic inn. As a chef's apprentice, he spent most of his time peeling potatoes and dicing onions. "I was so inept that after three days I knew the chef was going to fire me," he later remembered. One Sunday lunch, the kitchen ran out of potatoes. Because peeling and boiling potatoes was Wolfgang's job, the chef told him he'd better go home to his mother.

Stunned, the youth wandered through Villach, eventually finding himself on the banks of the Drava River. He

Panoramic view of Wörther See, where Wolfgang's mother Maria worked during the 1950s and 1960s. The Hotel Linde is located on the peninsula jutting out into the lake at the lower left.

An evening in Villach, Austria, where Wolfgang worked at several hotel restaurants as a teenager during the late 1960s.

contemplated ending his life, so great was his dread of returning to St. Veit and facing his father. "If I have to go home," he would recall thinking, "I'm going to have to kill myself." Finally, he thought of another alternative. He went back to the Hotel Post, where he lived in the basement. Only a few cooks knew of his presence there. They smuggled food to him, and in return he peeled potatoes.

After ten days, the hotel's owner discovered Wolfgang's hideout. Impressed by the youth's pluck, he sent Wolfgang to the nearby Park Hotel. There Wolfgang got another job.

While working in Villach, Wolfgang had an opportunity to attend a cooking school. He spent three years at the school, where his talent attracted notice. During his third year, he was selected to represent the school in a national culinary competition. He defeated 100 other cooks to capture the gold medal.

MICHELIN STARS

In 1900 the Michelin tire company published a guidebook for touring France by automobile, a mode of transportation that was still fairly novel. The guidebook included the locations of mechanics, fuel stations, and, not surprisingly, Michelin tire dealers. It also included listings for restaurants and inns.

A quarter century later, food became the primary focus of the Michelin guides. In 1926 the books began including restaurant reviews, using a star system to recognize excellence. The vast majority of restaurants received no stars. One star indicated very fine food. Two stars denoted outstanding cuisine that, in the opinion of the Michelin reviewer, justified a detour. A three-star rating was reserved for only the most exceptional restaurants, which were judged worthy of a special trip.

Over the years, Michelin guides expanded to include restaurants in European countries besides France and, later, to restaurants in various world cities. Receiving a Michelin star is still regarded as a high honor. The greatest chefs and most ambitious restaurateurs dream of garnering three Michelin stars, but the odds of ever realizing that dream are slim. Today, for example, fewer than 60 restaurants in Europe are awarded three stars each year.

Franz Berger, one of Wolfgang's teachers, advised the young man to continue his training in France. Wolfgang followed Berger's advice. In 1969, at the age of eighteen, he moved to the town of Les Baux, in southern France's Provence region, to work at a famous restaurant called L'Oustau de Baumanière. In addition to boasting three Michelin stars, L'Oustau de Baumanière was owned and operated by one of Europe's most innovative chefs, Raymond Thuilier.

Puck absorbed many essential lessons from Thuilier, a man he would credit as his greatest influence. Observing Thuilier "was like watching a great artist paint," Puck said. "I wanted to be like him. The way he cooked was from the

While working at the famous Provencal restaurant L'Oustau de Baumanière, Wolfgang trained with legendary French chef Raymond Thuilier.

heart. It was completely different from what I had learned. Everything was more about taste."

On his days off, Puck sometimes traveled to the nearby town of Salon-de-Provence with another young chef, Guy LeRoy. The two were captivated by a small restaurant there called Chez Gu, which featured an informal atmosphere and great pizza. Puck and LeRoy talked about owning their own establishment. "Our dream," Puck recalled, "was to make a little French restaurant with the pizza and the French cooking."

From L'Oustau de Baumanière, Puck moved to the Hotel de Paris in Monaco. He then cooked at Maxim's, an internationally renowned restaurant in Paris. These experiences broadened his skills. "They put you wherever they need you," Puck said of French chefs. He learned to use locally grown vegetables, locally caught fish, and locally made cheese to create an array of regional dishes.

As he grew more confident in his culinary skills, Puck increasingly thought about launching a restaurant with Guy LeRoy. The two friends were big fans of American movies, many of which featured rich characters and big cars. Imagining that everyone in the United States must be well-off, Puck and LeRoy began focusing their dreams on America.

Wolfgang's first good job in the United States was at La Tour, a restaurant atop the 20-story Indiana National Bank Building in Indianapolis. He worked there from 1973 to 1975.

CHAPTER THREE

THE AMERICAN DREAM

In 1973, at the age of twenty-four, Wolfgang Puck left his chef position at Maxim's in Paris and followed his dream to America. Puck and Guy LeRoy landed in New York City with only a few dollars in their pockets and speaking very little English. Fortunately, they had a contact. The son of a Paris hotel owner Puck knew ran a restaurant in New York, and he agreed to give Puck and LeRoy jobs.

A NOT-SO-GLAMOROUS LIFE

Life in America wasn't quite as Puck had imagined. He and LeRoy stayed in a grimy hotel, with cockroaches scurrying all over the bathtub. Puck found the noise and bustle of New York City overwhelming. Even worse, the restaurant where he worked had a simple, unimaginative menu. Puck quickly grew bored. He began looking for another job in a different city.

When he learned of an opening for a chef at a restaurant called La Tour, Puck applied. The restaurant was located in

Indianapolis, home of the Indy 500, and Puck was a big fan of auto racing. He imagined the capital of Indiana would as glamorous as Monte Carlo, a mecca for European racing. Offered the job at La Tour, Puck enthusiastically accepted.

But Indianapolis, Puck soon discovered, wasn't quite as cosmopolitan as Monte Carlo. Moreover, his bosses and coworkers at La Tour weren't impressed by the hotshot young chef who'd trained at Michelin-starred European restaurants. "It was as if everyone had been told to kick my butt and I had to say thank you," Puck recalled. "I had pans thrown at me, expletives."

Still, Puck remained at La Tour from 1973 until 1975, when he and Guy LeRoy bought a used Cadillac for $1,200 and headed west. They dubbed the road trip "La Voyage."

THE PLACE TO BE

The two friends ended up in Los Angeles. There they rented a cheap hotel room and looked for chef positions. Puck found work at a French restaurant, but he never got along with the manager. One day, the manager wrote out a menu and ordered Puck to cook it. "You wrote it; you cook it," Puck snapped as he walked out the door.

Puck was soon working at another French restaurant in Los Angeles. Called Ma Maison, it was decorated like a beach house, with Astroturf on the floor. Business was slow, and Puck's first weekly paycheck, for $300, bounced. Puck complained to Ma Maison's owner, Patrick Terrail, who offered him a 10 percent stake in the struggling restaurant. If

In French, Ma Maison means "My House."

you do a better job, Terrail told the young chef, Ma Maison will prosper. Puck accepted the challenge. He brought Guy LeRoy on board and set to work transforming the restaurant's menu.

During the early 1970s, food critics consistently disparaged the Los Angeles restaurant scene, calling the fare conventional and unimaginative. Chefs in the city's top restaurants didn't

Thanks to Wolfgang's unique food, as well as his talent for interacting with the rich and famous, Ma Maison soon became the place where the Los Angeles elite—such as Academy Award–winning actress Shelley Winters, pictured here—would meet to eat. By the late 1970s, Ma Maison was probably the most famous restaurant in the country.

take many chances; most seemed content to hew closely to the traditions of a given style of cooking.

Puck, on the other hand, was willing to experiment. At Ma Maison he pushed the boundaries of French cooking by incorporating elements of Italian and Asian cuisine. Within months, food critics had begun to take notice. After a solid review in the *Los Angeles Times* and glowing praise from *Gourmet* magazine, the restaurant's business took off. Diners flocked to Ma Maison, and among them were some of Hollywood's biggest stars.

Soon Puck and Terrail faced an interesting problem. Ma Maison didn't have nearly enough tables to accommodate the tsunami of customers eager to savor Puck's creative cooking. The two partners settled on a novel solution. The restaurant's phone number would be unlisted, so the general public wouldn't have any way to make reservations. The number would be given only to a select group of patrons: actors and auteurs, musicians and moguls, the famous and the wealthy and the powerful. Whether intended or not, this policy ensured that Ma Maison was the place to be for Hollywood's elite. In a town obsessed with status, being able to get a table at Puck's and Terrail's restaurant indicated membership on the A-list.

In October 1977 *People* magazine ran a piece about the restaurant and its exclusive clientele. "If someone dropped a bomb on this place right now," a motion picture executive quoted in the story said, "it would paralyze the entire entertainment industry." The buzz surrounding Ma Maison, and its twenty-seven-year-old head chef, only grew.

For Wolfgang Puck, the lesson was clear. "To be hot and talked about," he would note, "you have to do something new—that became one of my main philosophies." Of course, being hot and talked about never hurts the bottom line. Puck observed that Ma Maison was grossing just $18,000 a month when he started, but the figure eventually rose to $350,000.

RISING STAR

Ma Maison's success enabled Puck to move out of the cheap Los Angeles hotel where he and LeRoy had been staying. His new residence was a penthouse in the chic Hollywood Hills neighborhood.

Puck invited Marie France Trouillot, a woman he'd known in Paris, to join him in California. They married six months after her arrival.

The marriage didn't last. In 1979, after less than three years together, Puck and Trouillot divorced. Puck would admit that his focus on work had contributed significantly to the failure of his marriage.

PASTA PRIMER

Pasta is one of the most popular items on many restaurant menus. Most of us recognize fettuccine and spaghetti. But how about pappardelle and tagliatelle?

In his cookbook *Wolfgang Puck's Pizza, Pasta and More!* Puck lists and describes fifteen different types of noodles. Pappardelle is an inch-wide noodle that goes well with a chicken or meat sauce. Tagliatelle is a long, flat noodle, similar to fettuccine. Farfalle is shaped like little bowties. Tortellini (which is ring shaped) and cappelletti (shaped like a peaked hat) are types of pasta that can be stuffed with cheese or meat.

Puck's career was, however, going extremely well. His reputation continued to grow, and for that he largely had Patrick Terrail to thank. Terrail had encouraged his head chef to leave the kitchen and speak to the guests in Ma Maison's dining room. At first, Puck was tongue-tied in the presence of stars like Orson Welles, Elizabeth Taylor, Burt Reynolds, and Stevie Wonder. But he soon became more comfortable meeting and talking with celebrities. He would eventually count many as his friends.

Terrail also opened a cooking school, called Ma Cuisine, where Puck and other chefs taught classes. Puck's recipes became so popular that he was inspired to write his first cookbook, *Wolfgang Puck's Modern French Cooking for the American Kitchen*. It was published in 1981.

Wolfgang Puck could take satisfaction in all he'd accomplished in less than a decade in the United States. His culinary wizardry, combined with Terrail's business and marketing skills, had produced an enormously successful restaurant. Ma Maison had sparked a renaissance in the entire Los Angeles restaurant scene. Yet its influence extended well beyond L.A. "Together Wolfgang and I defined California cuisine," Terrail would say. That claim, while short on humility perhaps, wasn't far from the truth.

Puck and Terrail hadn't invented California cuisine—a style of cooking stressing the use of fresh, locally harvested ingredients—but they'd done as much as anyone to popularize it. Each day, Terrail obtained fresh produce for Puck's dishes from nearby farms and farmers markets. Puck continually adapted Ma Maison's menu according to which fruits, vegetables, and seafood were in season on the West Coast. This was a significant departure from the traditional restaurant model—especially for French restaurants, many of which would use ingredients shipped from far away (or some-times even frozen) in order to keep the same classic dishes always on the menu. But the freshness of the ingredients at Ma Maison allowed Puck to create marvelous flavors, and California cuisine caught on in a big way.

Puck could have rested on his laurels and continued his successful run at Ma Maison. But by the early 1980s, he was dreaming of another challenge: launching his own restaurant.

Puck's dream was encouraged by his girlfriend, Barbara Lazaroff. The two had met in 1979 at a Los Angeles night-club. Born and raised in New York City, Lazaroff—who was four years Puck's junior—had a background in set design and theater lighting. Their partnership would change the entire culinary world.

Wolfgang Puck poses in front of his famous West Hollywood restaurant Spago. The popularity of his restaurant among the wealthy and powerful of Los Angeles led to a nickname for Wolfgang: "chef to the stars."

CHAPTER FOUR

THE LAUNCHING OF SPAGO

I n 1981 Wolfgang Puck asked Patrick Terrail to be his partner in an Italian-style trattoria. Terrail agreed, but only on the condition that he receive 51 percent of the business. "No," Puck responded, "this is my idea." Terrail wouldn't budge, however, so Puck and Barbara Lazaroff decided to gamble on opening a restaurant without his help. Puck gave Terrail three months' notice that he would be leaving Ma Maison.

Unfortunately, word of Puck's plans had gotten out. Patrons at Ma Maison began asking the chef when his new restaurant would be opening. This deeply irritated Terrail, and one night he fired Puck on the spot. Ma Maison's head chef of six years was told to leave immediately.

FINANCING A DREAM

The unexpected firing slashed Puck's income, complicating his and Lazaroff's dream. Financing the new restaurant was already going to be difficult enough. That's because the build-

Wolfgang's girlfriend and business partner Barbara Lazaroff designed the interior of Spago. The restaurant opened in 1982. Thanks to Wolfgang's culinary ability and Lazaroff's penchant for publicity, Spago soon became the hottest spot in Hollywood.

Ma Maison's popularity declined after the departure of Wolfgang Puck. The restaurant closed in 1985.

ing Puck had found for the restaurant was on Sunset Strip, which was then a rather seedy part of West Hollywood. Banks declined to lend Puck money for a business in that neighborhood.

Puck appealed to longtime customers of Ma Maison and to people who took his cooking classes. Eventually, a dentist who loved Puck's cooking cosigned a bank loan for $60,000. About twenty other people invested a total of about $500,000 in the restaurant.

Puck and Lazaroff started renovations on the space, which had previously housed a dingy Armenian-Russian restaurant. "I wanted a bistro with simple food and plastic chairs," Puck said of his new venture. "Barbara had something more elaborate in mind, so we hit on an airy, beach house look."

Lazaroff designed the restaurant's interior. It was casual, with whitewashed walls and picture windows overlooking Sunset Boulevard. Lazaroff believed the restaurant could be akin to a theater, with the chefs as the actors onstage. She created an open kitchen where the customers could watch the cooks at work. Puck, the star, would be seen by everyone, which would give him an opportunity to interact with the crowd. "It was a huge PR stunt. You needed a certain kind of person to do it. His energy and concepts were groundbreaking," said designer Adam Tihany about Puck.

At first, Puck intended to name his new restaurant Mt. Vesuvio. A friend, the music composer Giorgio Moroder, suggested the name Spago, which means "string" or "spaghetti" in Italian. That name stuck.

WHAT IF NO ONE COMES?

Spago debuted on January 16, 1982. Barbara Lazaroff served as hostess, while Puck cooked on the grill. Kazuto Matsusaka, who had worked at Ma Maison, made salads. Mark Peel, who had also worked at Ma Maison, cooked pasta. Mary Bergin and Nancy Silverton were in charge of desserts. No one had tried cooking the menu before the big day, but Puck trusted his chefs.

He did, however, have one big worry: that no one would show up. Puck's concern turned out to be unfounded. "We just opened, and then I looked around, and the next thing the restaurant is full," he recalled. Puck counted 170 people the first night.

Puck's fans followed him from Ma Maison to Spago. Movie stars like Michael Caine, Sean Connery, Richard Gere, Michael Douglas, Jacqueline Bisset, Goldie Hawn, and Cher vied for tables. *Tonight Show* host Johnny Carson became a regular at Spago. So did actor-director Orson Welles, who loved chatting with Puck about food and wine.

Spago's success was immediate and overwhelming. During its first month, the restaurant made $20,000 in profit. Soon tables were booked three months in advance. In addition to the

A week before Spago opened, Puck wrote the menu on four sheets of paper. Mark Peel, a chef at Spago, had the pages framed. On Spago's twentieth anniversary, he presented them to Puck.

food, diners loved Lazaroff's elegant yet casual design. Fresh flower arrangements, colorful fabric on the bar, and the chefs cooking under theatrical lights created an exciting energy.

"The time was right," Puck said, "because people were really tired of these serious French restaurants with a snobby waiter and you're getting heavy sauces and everything. I think of Spago as my own house, and we make eating a party."

Spago definitely bore the imprint of Puck's experiences apprenticing at the finest European restaurants. "My philosophy was influenced by those years in the south of France," he noted.

> I believed that, whenever possible, a restaurant should represent the place where it is located. Los Angeles, with such a wonderful Mediterranean climate, was the ideal place to open a restaurant. Like southern France, the California climate allowed for a full year of growing, with season after season of incredible fruits and vegetables.

Puck went directly to farms and farmers' markets to find the freshest ingredients. A Sonoma farmer raised lambs to sell directly to him. Puck spent vacations in San Diego County at the Chino family farm, which used organic growing methods and, according to Puck, had tomatoes as tasty as the ones his mother grew in Austria.

Some of Spago's signature dishes became instant classics of California cuisine. These included roast chicken breast with goat cheese, duck pot stickers with daikon sprouts and plum-wine ginger sauce, and Sonoma baby lamb with braised greens and rosemary. But Spago became best known for Puck's gourmet take on an old favorite.

THE SCOOP ON TRUFFLES

Each year, Wolfgang Puck uses truffles to create dishes for the Academy Awards' Governors Ball and for the Spago menu. The menu for the 2005 Governors Ball featured truffled artichokes as well as Maine lobsters en croute with black truffles. One of the most popular Spago pizzas is white truffle with cheese. Yet many people have no idea what truffles are.

Truffles are irregularly shaped fungi that look something like warts. They range from the size of a walnut to the size of a person's fist. Since the time of the ancient Greeks and Romans, truffles have been eaten as delicacies and used as medicines. Because they are rare, they are among the most expensive of the world's natural foods. Black truffles cost as much as $1,000 a pound; white truffles, about $1,800 a pound.

Truffles grow underground, and dogs and female pigs are used to locate them by scent. Pigs often prove unreliable as truffle hunters, however, since they love to eat the fungi they find. Dogs, by contrast, can be trained to uncover truffles in exchange for a treat.

Stars of the television show Three's Company *Joyce DeWitt, Priscilla Barnes, and John Ritter sample one of Wolfgang's signature pizzas, 1983.*

Pizza!

When he'd worked at L'Oustau de Baumanière in southern France, Puck had made frequent trips to savor the pizza at Chez Gu. "Although we think of Italy as the land of pizza," Puck later wrote, "my influence comes from Provence, which also has a pizza tradition." At Chez Gu, pizzas were cooked in a wood-burning oven. They had crisp, thin crusts scented with the smoky flavor of the wood and were topped with just the right amount of sauce and cheese.

When he came to the United States, Puck was dismayed to find that "pizzas were prisoners of fast-food restaurants." American pizzas, in Puck's opinion, were too thick and doughy, with canned tomato sauce and greasy pepperoni.

Puck decided to create the perfect pizza at Spago. His colleagues thought this was a crazy idea. Serving pizza in a fine-dining restaurant was heresy.

Nevertheless, Puck went ahead with his idea. First, he needed a wood-burning oven, so he hired a German mason to build one in Spago's kitchen. Then he experimented, topping his crusts with unusual ingredients, such as goat cheese, sun-dried tomatoes, and duck sausage. A Greek pizza was topped with spinach, tomatoes, eggplant, feta, and pesto. Smoked-salmon pizza was created by accident when a customer wanted something to eat with his salmon. The restaurant was out of bread, so Puck brushed olive oil on a pizza crust and topped it with onion and caviar. Soon pizza was the most popular item

In order to get the authentic flavor he sought, Puck built a proper wood-burning oven in Spago's kitchen.

on Spago's menu. Puck helped this humble favorite achieve the status of a gourmet item, and it wasn't long before fine restaurants everywhere were serving pizza.

Building the new restaurant's business took thirteen-hour days, and many of Spago's employees quit in the face of the grueling schedule. But Puck never demanded a level of commitment from his employees that he wasn't willing to give. "He was the first to come and the last to leave," chef Jennifer Jasinski noted. "And it didn't matter how expensive or inexpensive a dish or ingredient was. . . . You made it with pride, and you made it right. He also had fun and has a great sense of humor with everything."

Puck's work ethic and commitment to serving great food impressed even his harshest critic. On a trip to America with his wife, Josef Puck visited Spago. Seeing just how successful the restaurant was, the father who had mocked his son's career choice changed his mind about men and cooking. "Men have to be in the kitchen," he declared.

Puck meets with guests at the original Spago on the Sunset Strip in West Hollywood, 1988. The innovative chef would eventually open more Spago restaurants in other cities.

CHAPTER FIVE

FROM CHEF TO ENTREPRENEUR

Spago confirmed Wolfgang Puck's genius as a chef, but more than great food is required for a successful restaurant. Puck and Lazaroff were novices at restaurant management, and Spago's runaway popularity soon spawned problems. The phones rang constantly but were rarely answered, reservations got mixed up, and invoices were lost. Five months after the restaurant opened, Puck realized he needed help. It came in the form of Thomas Kaplan, a manager at a restaurant called Croissant USA. After being hired by Puck, Kaplan worked nearly around the clock to get Spago organized. The feverish pace took a toll on his health, and Kaplan eventually landed in the hospital. But his efforts put Spago on a firm business footing.

Word of Spago's success spread, and a group of Japanese businesspeople asked Puck to open a Spago in Tokyo. Puck said no, so they told him they would open it without him. Because he hadn't trademarked the name, Puck couldn't prevent the group from building a replica, and they even hired a hostess who resembled Barbara Lazaroff. Fortunately for

Puck, the food at Spago Tokyo was terrible. When the Japanese group approached Puck again, he made a licensing deal and had his chefs train the Spago Tokyo cooks.

CHINOIS

By 1983, a year after the debut of the first Spago, Puck was ready for another challenge. At the time there were no fine-dining restaurants in Santa Monica, California. A group of investors wanted Puck to open another Spago there. "We were besieged with people wanting to invest in our next venture and to discourage them, I said we were just opening a Chinese restaurant," Puck recalled. "So then we had to do it."

Lazaroff, who had always wanted to design a Chinese restaurant, went wild renovating a former punk-rock club in Santa Monica. The interior had exposed brick, ceramic tiles, and bamboo accents. The dining plates were custom-made, and on display were two cloisonné cranes worth $25,000. Large vases were filled with silk flowers, and fans, dragon statues, and other antiques and Asian art adorned the restaurant. "It was very expensive to build Chinois for us: half the size for twice the price of Spago," Puck noted. "It was money well spent, looking back, but when you don't have it, it's a problem."

The renovations ultimately cost about $650,000, and the restaurant's opening was delayed for six months. Though it was busy from the start, Chinois (which means "Chinese" in French) was in debt for its first year and a half of operation. Lazaroff thought of Chinois as a painting. She spent a thousand dollars a week on fresh-cut flowers and had four hundred designer dresses to wear as hostess. Puck, who worried about the debt, considered selling the restaurant.

Chef Kazuto Matsusaka moved from Spago to Chinois, where the menu featured French- and California-influenced

Chinese cuisine. For inspiration, Puck used products from the Chinatown, Thai Town, and Little Tokyo neighborhoods of Los Angeles.

"We're not French, we're not Italian, we're not Asian, but we have influences from everywhere, and that is exactly what California is," Puck said. "I said the city has all this culture, so our cooking should have all this culture." Puck created dishes such as tempura sashimi and Mongolian lamb chops. This melding of flavors would set the stage for a style of cooking

When he was creating the cuisine at Chinois, Wolfgang found inspiration in Los Angeles's Chinatown neighborhood. He also blended Japanese and Thai staples with his traditional French fare to create an unusual new culinary style.

known variously as Pacific Rim, French-Asian, or fusion cuisine. It soon spread to other areas and restaurants.

A FRUITFUL PARTNERSHIP

Puck felt that with the opening of Chinois, he'd moved from chef to entrepreneur. At Spago he had taken a hands-on approach with every dish. Now he made Mark Peel head of Spago, which meant that he had to give up some control. "I think the most important thing when you grow is to hire good people . . . and make them feel that this is their own restaurant," Puck told an interviewer. Nevertheless, Puck spent long hours in both of his restaurants.

Lazaroff kept the same grueling schedule, dividing her time between Spago and Chinois. She brought glamour and a theatrical quality to her duties as hostess. For many diners, a meal at either establishment wouldn't be quite the same without Lazaroff. "Barbara makes it happen," said Alexander de Toth, the manager of an upscale restaurant in Dallas for which Puck has served as a menu consultant. "Whatever Wolf does in the kitchen, Barbara makes the world know about it."

Few could deny that the Puck-Lazaroff partnership worked spectacularly. In its first year, Chinois made about $2.3 million. The chef and the hostess/restaurant designer became major philanthropists. They established the Puck-Lazaroff Charitable Foundation to raise money for the Los Angeles Meals on Wheels, which provides hot meals for senior citizens and people with disabilities. "The most important thing is not that we just take, but we give back," Puck pointed out.

For a West Coast power couple, Lazaroff and Puck were rather sedate in their personal lives. They certainly weren't regulars on the Hollywood social scene. They shared a two-bedroom home in Los Angeles with a menagerie of pets: two cats, four dogs, two rabbits, and a cockatiel. Their lives revolved around the restaurants. In September 1983, after more than five years together, Lazaroff and Puck were quietly married.

Lazaroff did, however, plan a bigger wedding celebration. It was held in May 1984, in a setting that had special meaning for Puck: L'Oustau de Baumanière in Provence, where he had apprenticed with Raymond Thuilier. The three-day celebration was featured on the popular television show *Lifestyles of the Rich and Famous*.

STARDOM BECKONS

Puck had become more than just a successful chef and owner of two fine-dining restaurants. He was a sought-after celebrity. In 1986 he began appearing on ABC's *Good Morning America*. The guest spots introduced him and his cooking to television viewers all across the United States. Puck also starred in a video, titled *Spago Cooking with Wolfgang Puck*.

During this same period, Puck began mulling over another idea that had come to him courtesy of *Tonight Show* host Johnny Carson, a huge fan of Spago pizzas. "Johnny would take home 10 to 12 pizzas at a time," Puck recalled. "One day, I finally said, 'Johnny, what are you doing with all those pizzas?' He said, 'I put them in the freezer and pull them out when we're playing cards. They're just as good.'"

In 1957 the first frozen pizza, marketed by Celentano Brothers, became available in U.S. grocery stores.

Wolfgang displays some items from the line of frozen foods that he began sell-ing in the late 1980s.

Puck decided to develop a line of gourmet frozen pizzas for sale in supermarkets. He tested duck-sausage pizza, a Spago favorite, with a focus group, but it got a thumbs-down. Smoked salmon and prosciutto toppings didn't freeze well. Puck finally hit the jackpot with mixed cheeses, spicy-grilled chicken, and vegetables.

CHAPTER SIX

MANAGING SUCCESS

Wolfgang Puck's successes were mounting. The Wolfgang Puck Food Company was developed to market the chef's frozen pizzas, and a young executive named Selwyn Joffe was hired to head the company. "Joffe created a marketing plan that focused on the Wolfgang Puck brand," writer Juliette Rossant revealed in her book *Super Chef*. "He reasoned that the pizza had to be premium, made with the best quality ingredients, to separate it from the typical frozen pizza." After two years, the pizza business was making a profit.

In 1989 Puck and Lazaroff prepared to open a third fine-dining restaurant, this one in San Francisco's Prescott Hotel. The restaurant would be called Postrio, after its location on Post Street and the trio of chefs—Puck, and Anne and David Gingrass—who would be creating the menu and doing the cooking. As with Spago and Chinois, locally grown ingredients would have a major influence on the dishes served at Postrio. "The idea was a little bit of San Francisco, Chinatown, Little Italy and some traditional things to make sure it worked,"

In 1989, Wolfgang opened Postrio, a new restaurant in San Francisco's Prescott Hotel near historic Union Square.

Anne Gingrass said. Puck and the Gingrasses whipped up exquisite meals, such as Indonesian beef tartare with crispy garlic, crispy fried quail with apricot glaze, and Chinese duck with peach ginger vinaigrette.

New Horizons

In May 1989 Wolfgang Puck and Barbara Lazaroff welcomed their first child, a boy. They named him Cameron.

Puck's business ventures soon expanded from fine dining into casual dining. To promote the frozen-pizza business, Selwyn Joffe had decided to give away free samples at a Macy's department store in San Francisco. In 1991 the vice chairman of Macy's approached Joffe with the idea of a small eating area in Macy's Cellar. Called "Wolfgang Puck Express," it made $600,000 in its first year.

Joffe pitched the idea of a chain of cafés to Puck, who was skeptical. At the time, California Pizza Kitchen, with food modeled after Puck's Spago dishes, was growing rapidly. Puck knew that a chain could be quite lucrative, but he wasn't worried about money. He was confident that people loved his cooking enough to flock to any fine-dining venture he opened. Puck also thought it would be boring to be the head of a chain. "If I ever have to just attend board meetings and try to find new locations and meet with developers," Puck remarked, "I might as well go back to Austria."

Joffe persisted, however, arguing that a café chain would expose more diners to Puck's food and boost the frozen-pizza business. Eventually, Puck agreed. The first Wolfgang Puck Café was built on CityWalk at Universal City in 1993. Joffe

Wolfgang and Barbara show off their two-year-old son Cameron during a 1991 Christmas party held at Spago.

Wolfgang Puck has said that macaroons are his favorite food. His least favorite is peanut butter.

asked Barbara Lazaroff to design the cafés. She wanted them to be colorful and distinctive, so people would instantly recognize them as a Wolfgang Puck Café. The color scheme and pizza-shaped chairs mirrored the brand's frozen-pizza boxes. The menu was similar to Spago's offerings but moderately priced. According to the *New Yorker*, "Joffe envisioned Puck as 'the Armani of the food business,' modeling his approach on the fashion industry, where the high-priced label adds lustre to the brand, while the mass-oriented line reaps the profits." The idea worked, and soon Puck's casual-dining restaurants would be outselling the frozen-pizza division.

EUREKA AND GRANITA

Puck and Lazaroff had also set their sights on another restaurant concept. It would combine Puck's signature cuisine with a brewery. Puck and Lazaroff partnered with the owners of the Los Angeles Brewing Company in a venture called Eureka. The two-hundred-seat restaurant would have an on-site microbrewery. Lazaroff designed the space with her trademark creativity—and without regard to expense. Eureka cost about $8 million to set up. It opened in 1990. Unlike Puck's other restaurants, it didn't catch on immediately. In fact, Eureka lost about $20,000 a month.

The problems with Eureka didn't deter Puck from launching another restaurant around the same time. Granita, which means "Italian ice," opened in the beach community of Malibu. "The location is right by the ocean, so we think of it as an interpretation of the sea," Lazaroff said about her design for the restaurant. It was Mediterranean-themed, with two huge coral aquariums. As with Eureka, Lazaroff had plunged a lot of money into the creation of Granita.

The restaurant opened with a menu created by chefs from Spago. In its first few years, Granita lost money, largely because of problems beyond Puck and Lazaroff's control. The Los Angeles riots of 1992 spilled over into Malibu and scared customers away. Plus, heavy rains and mudslides periodically closed local roads. "You could have a Friday night where you had 250 reservations," Thomas Kaplan noted, "and then the rain comes and you lose the weekend."

HONORS AND SETBACKS

In 1991 Puck won the James Beard Foundation Award in the category of Outstanding Chef. The Beard Awards—which have been called the Oscars of the culinary world—are the food industry's highest honor. They are given in many categories, including chefs and restaurants, restaurant design, and books.

In May 1992 Eureka went into bankruptcy and closed after twenty-three months. The brewery beer, though widely praised, never made money in outlets other than the restaurant. The problem lay with the bottling process, which caused

Chef and food writer James Beard (1903–1985) was called "the Dean of American Cuisine." Beard appeared in one of the first televised cooking shows, 1946's *I Love to Cook*. He also founded the influential James Beard Cooking School.

the beer to turn cloudy. Dissatisfied customers routinely showed up at Eureka with six-packs of the beer and asked for a refund.

Puck, who owned about 10 percent of Eureka's debt, lost about $5 million. Many of his friends had also invested in the enterprise and lost money. Puck was angry and upset about this, but he learned a valuable lesson: Don't go into a business you don't understand and can't control. Before Eureka, Puck hadn't known anything about brewing, and it had cost him.

The Eureka debacle didn't cause Puck to stop taking risks, however. Soon he was looking to expand his dining empire into the unknown and uncharted culinary territory known as Las Vegas.

VIVA LAS VEGAS!

Puck often went to Las Vegas to take in boxing matches at the Mirage and Caesars Palace casinos. Las Vegas was world famous as a gambling mecca, but its cuisine was something less than world class. Cheap, all-you-could-eat buffets predominated.

Puck has said that he started a restaurant in Las Vegas purely by accident. In 1992 a developer named Sheldon Gordon contacted Puck and Lazaroff about putting a Spago in a mall called the Forum Shops, which Gordon was building next to Caesars Palace. Gordon's idea was to install a moving sidewalk that led from the entrance of the Mirage Hotel to the mall.

"I kept telling Sheldon Gordon, people wouldn't come to our restaurant and pay for food when casinos were giving it away free," Puck recalled. He and Lazaroff were thus doubtful that an investment in Las Vegas would pay off. "For people who had a flair for culinary arts," Lazaroff said, "coming

Tourists dine at Wolfgang Puck's Spago restaurant in the Forum Shops at Caesars Palace Hotel and Casino in Las Vegas.

to Las Vegas . . . was like going out West with a covered wagon and stew pot."

But Gordon persisted, eventually convincing Puck and Lazaroff that Las Vegas was ripe for a fine-dining venture. Spago Las Vegas opened in December 1992.

After the first week, Puck thought he'd made a huge mistake. The only events going on in Las Vegas during the week were rodeos. Puck joked that if he'd known there were going to be so many cowboys, he would have served ribs. Customers came into the restaurant and grabbed plates off the tables, expecting a buffet.

Finally, on New Year's Eve, the big Las Vegas shows resumed, a convention came to town, and Spago had lines out the door. Celebrities like Tony Danza and Arnold Schwarzenegger became customers. The restaurant went from serving three hundred dinners a night to serving two thousand dinners a night. Soon the Las Vegas Spago was making more money than the original Spago in West Hollywood.

In the beginning, finding fresh produce was difficult; Las Vegas is in the middle of the desert. Puck's employees had to drive a van to the Santa Monica Farmers' Market in California to bring back fruits and vegetables. Fresh fish and meat were flown into the Las Vegas airport. Soon a business developed in the area that was nicknamed "FedEx Cuisine." As word of Puck's success in Las Vegas spread, other chefs clamored to create high-end restaurants there. According to *Nation's Restaurant News*, Puck has been credited with being the "catalyst for the culinary whirlwind that has transformed the city into a fine-dining mecca."

THE RIGHT PEOPLE

As Puck's businesses grew, he had to redefine his role. He could no longer take a hands-on approach at his restaurants. He couldn't be in the kitchen of all his restaurants every day. But he did keep up a grueling schedule in order to ensure that all of the restaurants maintained the highest standards of quality. "He's not afraid to be a leader," Selwyn Joffe stated. "And his common sense is fabulous."

Puck gave his business and culinary teams a healthy measure of creative freedom. "Puck's ability to grow the company reflects his intuitive knack for hiring the right people," observed Thomas Kaplan, who became a partner in Puck's fine-dining division, "training them well and then empowering them to do their jobs. He's a micromanager . . . who's able to teach his philosophies to management and get that down to the unit level."

According to Puck, paying staff what they deserve, giving them a stake in the business, giving them credit for their successes, and treating them well are all essential ingredients to retaining great employees. Others who know Puck say that his genuine caring for customers, clients, and especially his employees is a huge part of his growing success. "A number of years ago," Kaplan told an interviewer in 2000, "one of the chefs' houses burned down. The very next day Barbara and [Wolfgang] were there with clothes, food and money to help him. So many employees have stayed with him for so long—more than five or 10 years. In a business with a huge turnover, that's pretty amazing."

Wolfgang Puck poses with legendary chef Julia Child (1912–2004) at a 1998 event. Julia Child was one of the original celebrity chefs, thanks to her bestselling 1961 cookbook Mastering the Art of French Cooking and to television shows like The French Chef and In Julia's Kitchen with Master Chefs.

CHAPTER SEVEN

EXPANDING THE EMPIRE

By the mid-1990s, Wolfgang Puck had more on his plate than most mere mortals could manage. His restaurants included Spago in Los Angeles and Spago Las Vegas, Chinois, Postrio, and Granita. Then there were the Wolfgang Puck Cafés and the Wolfgang Puck Express, not to mention the frozen-pizza business. To keep all these ventures running, Puck logged sixteen-hour workdays. Each month he flew to New York to do a guest cooking spot on *Good Morning America*. He also crisscrossed the country promoting his and Lazaroff's various ventures. Once his jet lag was so overwhelming that Puck fell asleep in the middle of a radio interview.

As if he weren't busy enough, in 1994 Puck became a father again when Lazaroff gave birth to another son, Byron James. By this time, the family had moved into a mansion in Los Angeles. But Puck had little time to relax there. He was on the road up to two hundred days out of the year.

Nevertheless, Puck ventured into a new business in 1995: hawking kitchenware. "My field extends from the kitchen to the dining room, to the outside dining—whatever is enter-taining," Puck said about his decision to put his name on a line of cooking products. "I can see myself in Target with the 'Wolfgang Puck Collection.' "

In the end, though, Puck sold his branded cookware not in stores but on television. He began with QVC and then, after some disputes with that company's management, moved to the Home Shopping Network (HSN). On HSN, Puck demonstrated his recipes using his signature line of blenders, electric grills, and bakeware. "Merchandising is where I make the most money for the least effort," the chef candidly admitted. "Now I go to Tampa six times a year to do 16 hours of live television each visit. It's grueling work, but it's worthwhile."

A FORCE IN THE CATERING BUSINESS

In 1995, after his much-touted debut as host of the Academy Awards' Governors Ball, Puck was approached with yet anoth-er business proposition. Carl Schuster, the head of a food serv-ice and catering company called Restaurant Associates, want-ed to develop a national catering company using Puck's name. Puck asked Schuster to create a marketing plan, which the two men reviewed one weekend. Puck was satisfied, and he and Schuster sealed their deal with a handshake.

Schuster became president of Wolfgang Puck Catering & Events Group. Puck and Lazaroff were vice presidents. The

In 2000, Puck sold more than $10 million worth of cooking accessories on the Home Shopping Network. The following year, that figure topped $15 million.

Thanks to his insistence that catered meals should reflect the same quality as meals served in his restaurants, Wolfgang's catering company, started in 1995, has been wildly successful. Wolfgang Puck Catering & Events Group has provided food at major events like the Oscar and Grammy awards ceremonies, as well as for private parties and occasions like the 2011 wedding of reality show star Kim Kardashian and basketball player Kris Humphreys.

company's goal was not only to cater big events like the Oscars, but also to gain loyal customers who wanted parties catered in their homes. As always, Puck's emphasis was on the food. "We approach the catering just like we do the restaurant," he explained.

If you go to hotels, they plate the food in the afternoon, then put it in hot boxes and let it sit for hours, then heat it up and serve it. Nothing is really hot, and everything tastes the same. But we treat every event

AN OLYMPIAN EFFORT

Wolfgang Puck has served as an adviser to the American team that competes in the World Culinary Olympics. With up to fifty countries and more than 1,100 chefs taking part, this is the largest cooking competition in the world.

In accepting an invitation to advise the U.S. team, Puck believed he could bring something important to the table: clarifying the team's ideas about the meaning of American food. "Listen, perhaps this should be our style," Puck says of his role. "This is what American should be."

Puck's work may well have made a difference. In 2009 the U.S. team placed second in the World Culinary Olympics, losing to Switzerland by just six points. The U.S. team served such American delights as herb-infused turkey breast with mushroom stuffing and cranberry johnny cake to 175 diners.

as if it was one of our restaurants. We serve the food hot and fast. . . . Word of mouth is our biggest advertisement. We don't use magazines or television. The most important ad for us is that everyone must go home happy.

MORE FINE DINING

In 1996 Puck and Lazaroff opened another fine-dining establishment, ObaChine, on North Beverly Drive in Beverly Hills. Lazaroff filled the two-story, two-hundred-seat restaurant with artifacts from Vietnam, Thailand, Singapore, and Hong Kong. She valued the artwork at about $100,000. The menu emphasized Chinese, Japanese, Korean, Malaysian, and Thai dishes, with Puck's signature flair and emphasis on fresh ingredients. Critics claimed that diners needed a translator to read the menu, although reviews were generally positive.

A third Spago opened in Chicago in 1996. Puck put his younger brother, Klaus, in charge there. Klaus Puck had worked for many summers at the original Spago as well as at his brother's other fine-dining restaurants. Later, he'd studied restaurant and hotel management at Cornell University.

In 1997 Wolfgang Puck and Barbara Lazaroff spent $4 million to open another Spago, in Beverly Hills. The menu featured updated Spago classics, but Puck also added dishes from his homeland of Austria. These included Wienerschnitzel (a dish made with veal cutlets) and Kaiserschmarrn (a dessert of caramelized pancakes with plum, apple, or strawberry sauce on top). As a child, Puck had been especially fond of Kaiserschmarrn.

It had been fifteen years since the debut of the original Spago, but Puck managed to keep diners enthralled with his innovative cuisine. Food critics raved about Spago Beverly Hills. A reviewer for the *New York Times* wrote that Puck's marrow soup was one of the best dishes she'd ever eaten. A fifth Spago was opened later in 1997, in Palo Alto, California.

That same year, Puck and Lazaroff received the Innovator of the Year Award from *Nation's Restaurant News*. "Every year we seek out a unique operator who has impacted the industry across any spectrum of innovation," said James C.

Puck's first business motto was "Where food meets life." In the late 1990s, he changed his motto to "Live, love, eat!"

Doherty, editor and publisher of the journal. "This year's recipients embody the true meaning of innovation."

Puck was lauded for his culinary influence and Lazaroff for her restaurant design. Both were cited for their team-work. The ever-modest Puck claimed that hard work and a dedication to pleasing customers, not a desire to innovate, was what drove him. But there was no denying that Puck had been a culinary groundbreaker, from his introduction of pizza and wood-burning ovens into fine-dining restaurants to his expansion of the concept of fast food with his cafés. "What he did in the '80s was really innovative," observed award-winning chef Josiah Citrin, "but now he is cross-pollinating cuisines. That he's been so successful for such a long period of time is amazing."

The James Beard Foundation Award judges agreed. In 1998 the Beard Foundation again gave Puck the Outstanding Chef of the Year Award. He became the only chef to win the coveted award twice.

CHAPTER EIGHT

GROWING PAINS

As the new millennium approached, Wolfgang Puck presided over an expanding culinary empire. With the opening of a second Chinois, a second Postrio, and Trattoria del Lupo (an Italian restaurant in Las Vegas), the Wolfgang Puck Fine Dining Group operated a dozen establishments.

Puck's catering business was growing fast. So was his packaged-food business. In addition to its flagship frozen pizzas, the Wolfgang Puck Food Company offered frozen lasagna, ravioli, tortellini, and cannelloni. In 1999 a new line of premium canned soups began appearing on West Coast supermarket shelves.

Puck maintained a brutal schedule, often working a hundred hours a week. Still, he couldn't possibly stay on top of all of his far-flung ventures. Puck had to trust his longtime chefs and staff. He devoted most of his efforts to making sure the less established enterprises flourished. "I always go to the newer restaurants," Puck said. "When the restaurants do really well, it's just like having children; when they need me, I go. If they don't need me as much, I don't go as much."

Wolfgang and Barbara pose in their new restaurant, Wolfgang Puck Café at the Walt Disney World Resort in Florida, September 1997.

TAKING STOCK

In July 1999 Puck turned fifty. He marked the milestone by hosting a fund-raiser for the University Hospital of Cleveland's Ireland Cancer Center, which ensures that patients receive cutting-edge care. Twenty-seven fellow chefs donated their time for the event, and they surprised Puck with a birthday cake. Puck later celebrated a celebrity-studded birthday party at the Bellagio in Las Vegas.

Puck decided to cut back on his insane work hours and spend more time with his wife and sons. Cameron was now ten, and Byron five. Puck took the boys to school each morning and swam with them in the afternoons. A pizza night might follow. Like his father, Cameron displayed an early interest in good food—Puck would boast that his elder son could tell the difference between homemade and store-bought pasta by age two—and the boy loved to invite friends to the house to make pizzas. On these occasions, Puck would supervise. On other nights, the chef cooked for his family rather than for restaurant guests. Puck savored these moments. "I changed back into my work clothes, put on an apron, and started to dig through the cupboards and refrigerator," he recalled of one such night.

> Cameron and Byron watched in anticipation as I put water on to boil for pasta and began washing vegetables for the salad. As they quizzed me about each step—why I salted the water, how to tell when the noodles are ready—I remembered watching my mother when I was a boy and asking the same questions.

CONTROVERSY

The tranquility and satisfaction Puck found at home was tempered somewhat by a very public controversy. It involved ObaChine, Barbara Lazaroff, and allegations of racial and cultural insensitivity.

In 1998 Puck and Lazaroff opened ObaChine Seattle. It joined two other ObaChine restaurants—the original in Beverly Hills, and a second location in Phoenix, Arizona. Almost from the outset, ObaChine Seattle ran into problems. Behind the restaurant's reception desk, and visible from the sidewalk, was a vintage poster. It depicted a Chinese man in a servant's jacket, carrying a cup of tea; his hair was tied in a long braid, and his eyes had an exaggerated slant. The same poster had adorned the Beverly Hills ObaChine since its debut, attracting little notice. In Seattle, the story was different. Seattle's larger Asian community was more sensitive to the fraught history of Asians in the United States. In the late nineteenth and early twentieth century, Chinese immigrants had faced decades of severe discrimination. During World War II, Japanese Americans on the West Coast were rounded up and sent to internment camps.

Given this context, many people in Seattle's Asian-American community found the poster in ObaChine—which represented an early-twentieth-century stereotype of Chinese men—to be offensive. The restaurant was boycotted. Protesters stood outside and chanted, "ObaChine is obscene! Sushi, yes! Slant eyes, no!"

Lazaroff, who had designed ObaChine Seattle and chosen the poster, felt personally attacked. She flew to Seattle to discuss the situation with Rob Chew, director of the Wing Lake Asian Museum. But instead of agreeing to remove the poster, Lazaroff dug in her heels. She told reporters that the Wolfgang Puck companies were dedicated to ethnic diversity, but she insisted that the poster was art, not a realistic portrayal of an Asian-American person.

Chew wasn't placated by that explanation. "I'm a lifelong Seattlite," he said, "and nothing in my memory has triggered such strong reactions in the local community." The protests continued, eventually spreading to the Phoenix ObaChine.

Puck never commented publicly on the controversy. But in late May of 1999, all three ObaChines were quietly closed.

PUCK, INC.

Puck's dining empire, meanwhile, was expanding in other directions. From 1997 to 2000, Wolfgang Puck Grand Cafés were built in Florida, Illinois, Colorado, and California. The

Grand Cafés were larger versions of Puck's original cafés. As usual, Lazaroff took charge of their design. She used bright-colored tiles to create a distinctive look.

WOLFGANG PUCK'S STRATEGIES FOR SUCCESS

Puck wasn't an instant sensation. He worked long and hard, adhering to his five strategies for success:

1) **Don't ever quit.** Josef Puck had told his son that he was good for nothing. The future chef had once stood on a bridge and contemplated ending it all. But he refused to give up on his dream—and his early failures made him work harder.

2) **Keep perspective.** Puck's philosophy was to make his customers happy by offering great food and service, but he was also able to handle bad reviews and think beyond the day-to-day challenges to future endeavors.

3) **Balance artistry with business.** Puck's culinary touch made him a top-notch chef, but he also paid close attention to financial matters.

4) **Build a strong team.** Puck trusted his staff and employees, gave them credit for jobs well done, and empowered them to succeed.

5) **Study what works and then keep improving.** Puck constantly grows as a chef and an entrepreneur, learns from his mistakes, and isn't afraid to make changes.

Puck signed an agreement to develop restaurants world-wide for the Walt Disney Company. In 2001 a huge 350-seat café opened at Disneyland, the company's theme park in Anaheim, California. Its interior featured an undersea theme, and a giant statue of King Neptune towered over the entrance. Unfortunately, the project fell victim to bad timing—the terrorist attacks of September 11 led to a precipitous decline in visitors to all Disney parks—and the Disneyland café was shuttered after just eight months.

By this time Puck's business had grown so large and unwieldy that it had to be divided into three divisions: the Wolfgang Puck Fine Dining Group, which oversaw the high-end restaurants; Wolfgang Puck Catering & Events; and Wolfgang Puck Worldwide, responsible for Puck's kitchenware, food lines, and the Wolfgang Puck Express and Wolfgang Puck Café casual dining outlets.

Over the years, Puck had made many forays into television. In addition to his regular spots on *Good Morning America*, he'd appeared on game shows, been interviewed by all the major talk show hosts, and even had guest roles playing himself on sitcoms such as *Who's the Boss?*, *Frasier*, and *The Simpsons*. But in 2000 the chef got his own TV series with the Food Network. Executives at the network, which debuted in 1995, had long wanted Puck to star in a show. But the Food Network is based in New York City, and Puck balked at more travel to the East Coast. Eventually the Food Network came to him, arranging to film the series *Wolfgang Puck in Hollywood*.

Wolfgang Puck became a U.S. citizen in 1999.

By the late 1990s, Wolfgang had become a pop culture icon, appearing as himself on several popular television shows. Here he stars in an episode of the NBC sitcom Frasier, *with the show's stars David Hyde Pierce (as Dr. Niles Crane) and Kelsey Grammer (as Dr. Frasier Crane).*

At the time his TV show premiered, Puck had a new offering on bookstore shelves. The cookbook—his fourth—was titled *Pizza, Pasta and More!* Puck said the book sprang from his desire to write recipes that would bring families together in the kitchen. "If we are all sitting around the pool," Puck said about his own family, "we don't really say much, we swim or whatever. Cooking together in the confined space of the kitchen, the boys feel much freer to talk. We learn about what's going on in their lives, and they learn about food."

GIVING BACK

Helping the less fortunate was also a family affair. As they'd done since 1982, Puck and Lazaroff continued hosting the

Wolfgang's Food Network show debuted in 2000 and ran for five years.

American Wine & Food Festival, which benefited the Los Angeles Meals on Wheels program. The first festival was held in the parking lot of Spago in Hollywood, but the enormous growth in the event's popularity necessitated a move to a larger area—the back lot at Universal Studios where European street sets are located. By this time, the American Wine & Food Festival had raised more than $5 million.

The Puck-Lazaroff Charitable Foundation won kudos for its administrative efficiency: 99 percent of the money collected went directly to charity, according to *Forbes* magazine. Others familiar with Puck's charitable endeavors had high praise for him personally. "He's a very gentle person. He's

In 2002 Wolfgang Puck's Food Network series won a Daytime Emmy for Outstanding Service Show.

very committed to the needs of the elderly," said Sister Alice Marie Quinn, a volunteer with the Los Angeles Meals on Wheels. "His staff are all very committed as well."

Puck was also a perennial volunteer at another benefit for Meals on Wheels—the annual tribute to James Beard held at New York City's Rockefeller Center. Writer and restaurant critic Gael Greene observed Puck there, and she lauded the famous chef's enthusiasm and approachability. "He stands at his station and talks to everyone," Greene wrote. "So many people seem to know him. Wherever he is, it's fun to be there."

ENDINGS

In 2001 the enterprise that had catapulted Wolfgang Puck and Barbara Lazaroff to superstardom in the restaurant world—the original Spago in Hollywood—closed down after nineteen years in operation. To the very end, the ground-breaking Spago was making food that restaurant critics and ordinary diners alike savored. Ultimately, however, the restaurant fell victim to the success of its sister Spago in Beverly Hills, which opened in 1997. Gradually, the celebrity clientele had gravitated to the Beverly Hills location, robbing the original of much of its luster.

The fate of Puck and Lazaroff's first restaurant seemed emblematic of their relationship, which was floundering. Despite his efforts to spend more time with his family, Puck was constantly preoccupied with his business ventures. Lazaroff has intimated that she resented the toll this took on their domestic life. For her part, though, Lazaroff had started her own Beverly Hills design firm.

In December 2002, Lazaroff filed for a divorce. After nineteen years, Wolfgang Puck's second marriage had come to an end.

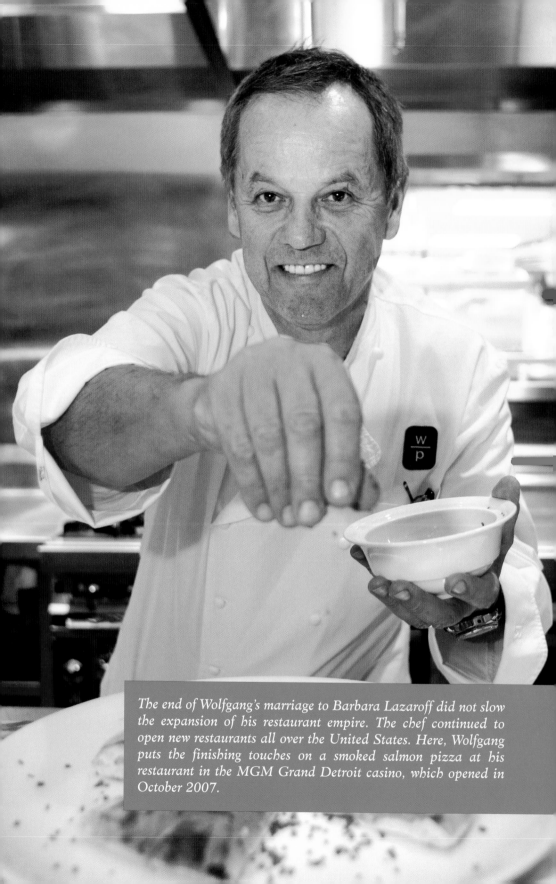

The end of Wolfgang's marriage to Barbara Lazaroff did not slow the expansion of his restaurant empire. The chef continued to open new restaurants all over the United States. Here, Wolfgang puts the finishing touches on a smoked salmon pizza at his restaurant in the MGM Grand Detroit casino, which opened in October 2007.

CHAPTER NINE

BALANCING ACT

At the time of their divorce, Puck and Lazaroff had been business partners for twenty-one years, enjoying incredible professional success together. Despite the breakup, Lazaroff would remain a partner in Puck's restaurant empire.

That empire continued to grow. Spago Maui, opened in 2001 in Hawaii, soon emerged as Puck's most profitable restaurant anywhere. In 2002 Puck opened a restaurant called Vert in the Hollywood & Highland Center. It was a brasserie, a relaxed, upscale French restaurant serving hearty food. Though popular in France, brasseries were uncommon in the United States. Vert, French for "green," was the first in what Puck hoped would be a chain of brasseries named for colors. The idea, however, never caught on.

Wolfgang Puck Express, Puck's fast-casual concept, had grown to fifteen restaurants. Most were located in airports and Gelson's Market grocery stores in California. Puck continually worked on the design and the food. In 2003 he introduced ordering and paying at a host podium. Puck also experimented with adding more value specials, a dessert station, more gourmet coffees, and more customized dishes for dietary needs and tastes. "The most difficult thing for me," he said, "is the inexpensive restaurant like Wolfgang Puck Express—it is easier to cook with something expensive. It's hard to create a great meal for $10. For me that is much harder than opening a fine-dining restaurant. I have to work at it all the time." Puck's signature sauces, soups, breads, and dressings were made in Arizona and then flown to the restaurants. This helped keep the quality and taste consistent.

FOOD FOR TRAVELERS

Puck also turned his attention to the gastronomic tribulations of airline travelers. "The airlines," he joked, "are a great way to be on a diet. The more you fly, the more you can be on a diet." Puck sought to offer a little relief by bringing his gourmet touch to in-flight meals. In 2003 he signed a deal with LSG Sky Chefs, which catered food for 260 airlines, to provide gourmet breakfasts, lunches, and dinners. Choices included some Puck favorites, such as Chinois chicken salad and a smoked turkey sandwich with spinach. Since temperature and pressure changes make food taste different in a plane, Puck had to test many dishes.

Air travelers would soon have the chance to enjoy some of Puck's food while they waited for their flights. In 2004 Puck signed a deal with HMSHost—a worldwide provider of food and beverages for the travel industry—to operate Wolfgang Puck Express outlets in about thirty airports. "We feel that the Wolfgang Puck menu is a great fit for travelers because of its freshness and diversity," said Patrick Carroll, HMSHost's vice-president of concepts. "Today's travelers are looking for more than typical fast-food meals. They want

The exterior of a Wolfgang Puck Express in Nashville, Tennessee.

fresh, meaningful culinary experiences, and Wolfgang's dynamic creations are truly special."

New Beginnings

Despite his whirlwind professional life, Puck found time for another romantic relationship. Ethiopian-born Gelila Assefa had come to the United States in 1986 to study fashion at Los Angeles Trade Technical College. In the 1990s, while trying to launch her own couture store, Assefa had worked as a hostess at Spago. She and Puck met in 1997 and began dating after his divorce. In 2003 they bought a house in Beverly Hills together and set about redesigning it for a family.

Wolfgang and Gelila Assefa attend the Academy Awards ceremony. They began dating in 2003.

That same year Puck's weekly cooking column, Wolfgang Puck's Kitchen—distributed by Tribune Media Services—debuted in thirty newspapers. Puck offered expert tips, guidelines, and recipes tailored to the home cook. He said his goal was to change home cooking. His columns often included a dash of the whimsical—topics included "Celebrate Asparagus" and "A Special Treat for the Queen of the House," which provided pampering tips for Mother's Day—but Puck also gave his readers a few culture and history lessons. For example, his column on Kaiserschmarrn (which means "emperor's mishmash" in German) explained that the dessert was first prepared for the Austrian emperor Franz Josef, who reigned for almost sixty-eight years.

With Restaurant 20.21, Puck created his first museum-based restaurant. It opened in the Walker Art Center in Minneapolis, Minnesota. Pairing a culinary destination with a cultural attraction seemed like an inspired idea to Puck. The museum debuted its $135 million expansion in 2005, renovating the dining area as well.

In 2005 Puck also returned to Indianapolis, where he'd held one of his first jobs in America, to create a restaurant at the remodeled Indianapolis Museum of Art. It was simply called Puck's. The venue had lofty ceilings and immense white columns, framing huge windows that overlooked the museum's Sutphin Fountain. Chef Brad Gates, who hailed from Fort Wayne, Indiana, had trained with Puck. Even

In 2008 Campbell's Soup Company bought Wolfgang Puck's $22 million organic soup business. Puck continues to create the recipes.

CHEFS AS TV STARS

It may be surprising that cooking, which is all about smells and tastes, plays well on television, a visual and auditory medium. Yet some food shows have achieved great popularity, catapulting the chefs they spotlight to fame.

In 2010 the Food Network averaged a million viewers a day. The network's success spawned a spin-off, called the Cooking Channel, which airs shows such as *Two Fat Ladies* (featuring Jennifer Paterson and Clarissa Dickson Wright) and *Emeril Live* (featuring Emeril Lagasse). CBS airs *The Rachael Ray Show*, a popular daytime offering. As of 2011, Fox's *Hell's Kitchen* with Gordon Ramsay had run nine seasons. Bravo's blockbuster *Top Chef* proved so popular that it led to three spin-offs, including *Top Chef: All Stars*, for which Wolfgang Puck served as a guest judge.

Puck has nothing against a good cooking show. But he feels that television gives many aspiring chefs unrealistic expectations about achieving culinary stardom. "People want to be everything in two years," he noted on the ABC News program *Nightline*. "They think I started to cook, two years later I opened Spago, then I had the TV show, and here I am. They don't want to learn the profession. It takes a long time."

In recent years, television stardom has made trained chefs and restaurateurs like Gordon Ramsay, Bobby Flay, and Tom Colicchio into nationally recognized celebrities.

though Puck wasn't actually in the kitchen, his entrées ruled the menu. As always, dishes such as salad with roasted beets and steamed salmon Hong Kong style were made from fresh, local ingredients.

ACCOUNTANTS AND ARTISTS

To expand the number of his restaurants successfully, Puck—and his staff—needed to be both accountants and artists. "It's difficult to find talented chefs who can also be talented businessmen," Puck noted. "The margins are narrow. It's a labour intensive business and you have to watch costs. I'm not talking about using cheap ingredients, which is suicide. You have to watch waste and ensure that people are nice to each other so you don't have problems with employees."

More than ever, Puck relied on a team of dedicated partners, many of whom owned a share in the growing business. Puck compared himself to a football coach. "I make my team play together the way I want them to play," he said.

Wolfgang and Gelila Assefa Puck attend a 2009 event with their children Oliver and Alexander. After dating for about five years, Wolfgang and Gelila married in 2007.

CHAPTER TEN

LIVING, LOVING, EATING

Wolfgang Puck and Gelila Assefa's first son, Oliver, was born on July 17, 2005. A second son, Alexander, arrived on December 21, 2006. The famous actor Sidney Poitier and his wife were the godparents of both children.

"I am the happiest woman on the planet. I feel like he's a gift," Assefa said of Puck. "I'm lucky to have him in my life."

In order to focus on motherhood, Assefa walked away from a demanding job in fashion design. At the same time, she wanted an outlet for her artistic impulses, so in 2006 she began her own line of handbags, called Gelila. "We all have this energy that needs to be addressed in some creative way," she said. "The handbag line is manageable, to where I can be a mother to my children. That's my first responsibility."

A CUT ABOVE

Around the same time Gelila Assefa launched her handbag line, Wolfgang Puck debuted yet another innovative restaurant concept. Located at the Beverly Wilshire, a Four

Seasons Hotel in Beverly Hills, CUT was a steakhouse—with a cutting-edge twist. It featured the best-quality beef from the United States, Australia, and New Zealand, along with an extensive and imaginative menu of Puck-created salads and appetizers. These inspired offerings included Kobe steak sashimi with spicy radishes; maple-glazed pork belly with Asian spices, watercress, sesame-orange dressing, and a Fuji apple compote; filet mignon carpaccio with celery hearts, truffle hollandaise, and black truffles; and many more.

Puck's new restaurant drew big crowds and rave reviews. The influential food critic John Mariani gave CUT his "Restaurant of the Year" award. *Bon Appétit* rated CUT as one of the top three steakhouses in the entire United States. The restaurant soon garnered a coveted Michelin star.

Puck had taken the concept of the steakhouse to a higher level. And he followed up on the success of the Beverly Hills CUT by opening versions in other cities: Las Vegas, Singapore, London. These, too, were very popular.

STAYING FRESH

CUT's success notwithstanding, by 2006 Puck had initiated an effort to better integrate the various components of his multifaceted culinary empire. As they expand, many organizations develop what has been called a "silo mentality"—with different divisions failing to communicate with one another. This situation can lead to missed opportunities, inefficiency, and other problems. Puck's empire had grown so big so fast that he wondered whether he'd charted the best future course. He hired a branding and design consulting firm to help link Wolfgang Puck Fine Dining, Wolfgang Puck Catering & Events, and Wolfgang Puck Worldwide, while allowing them to grow in their different directions.

A new logo was created that tied the three divisions and their various products and restaurants together. The logo consisted of a thin box that enclosed "WOLFGANG" in small white type above "PUCK" in large green letters. The logo capitalized on the chef's famous name, with a color palette suggestive of fresh food.

Wolfgang Puck Express, the casual dining chain, was renamed Wolfgang Puck Gourmet Express. The catering division continued its push to move into museums and cultural centers across the country. But what still drove the entire organization was the Fine Dining Group, which spotlighted Puck's ever-evolving cuisine. "It's the lab and the creative engine," said Thomas Kaplan, senior partner of the Fine Dining Group. "We can't let it become generic. We want to stay cutting edge and not get complacent."

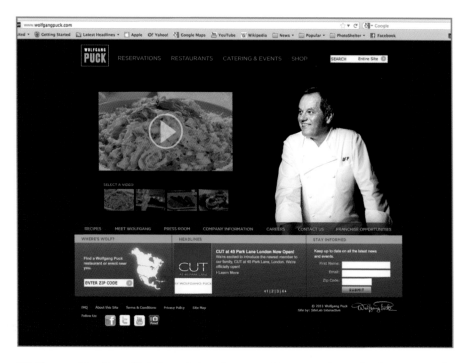

Wolfgang Puck's official website (www.wolfgangpuck.com) showcases the chef's green and white logo in the upper left.

That attitude defined Wolfgang Puck himself. In 2007 Puck received a major honor: he was named Fine Dining Legend by *Nation's Restaurant News*. But this legend wasn't about to rest on his laurels. "I still believe I got this award 20 years too early," Puck said in his acceptance speech. "I am still learning every day about this business."

POWER COUPLE

In July 2007, ten years after they'd first met, Wolfgang Puck and Gelila Assefa were married on the Italian island of Capri. Not surprisingly, food played a leading role in the three-day celebration, which included a 58th-birthday bash for the groom. The 250 guests who attended the wedding reception enjoyed a menu created by Puck's own catering team. It featured such delicacies as seafood ravioli and smoked-tuna carpaccio. The five-tier wedding cake was made with fresh Capri lemons. "It was beyond my dream wedding," the 38-year-old Assefa gushed.

At the outset of his third marriage—and with two young children—Puck seemed to take a somewhat different perspective on his life. The longtime workaholic now touted the benefits of balance. "Having grown a little bit older and

In 2009, when *Forbes* magazine published a list of the most successful married celebrity entrepreneurs, Wolfgang and Gelila Assefa Puck made the cut. Other power couples on the list included superstar entertainers Jay-Z and Beyoncé; soccer star David Beckham and singer-turned-fashion-designer Victoria Beckham; and actress Salma Hayek and apparel magnate François-Henri Pinault.

In 2008 the Culinary Institute of America honored Wolfgang Puck as Chef of the Year. The institute recognized Puck for his wide-ranging impact on the culinary world.

maybe a little bit wiser, I think success is a 50/50 proposition," Puck told an interviewer. "It is half business and half your private life. If you are really successful in business but have a bad marriage and the kids are not doing well, you know, you are not a happy person."

Puck made an effort to enjoy time with his wife and their children, Oliver and Alexander. Yet he maintained a pace of work that would exhaust most people half his age. Puck's wife understood completely. In fact, she shared his drive to continually achieve new professional successes. "Could you imagine," she asked a reporter rhetorically, "if I didn't work and just sat at home and waited for him once the kids went to bed?"

A successful entrepreneur in her own right, Gelila Assefa Puck built a flourishing handbag business. Her purses and pocketbooks, manufactured in South Africa, are decidedly high-end. Made from springbok and Nile crocodile skins, they sell for $2,500 to $30,000. Assefa Puck also designs textiles. Her fabrics are handmade by Ethiopian weavers, and she feels they convey the joy of Africa.

A large part of why she and her husband work so hard, Assefa Puck believes, is that they are both first-generation immigrants. They share the big dreams and the drive to achieve that have characterized countless people drawn to America's shores. Of course, the Pucks both love what they do as well.

CULINARY MISSIONARY

Wolfgang Puck has always taken joy in great food, and he spreads that joy with the zeal of a missionary. Puck presides over a culinary empire that generates about $350 million in annual revenue. He employs upwards of four thousand people worldwide and has a hundred restaurants to his name. And yet, if someone wants him to cater a private party—and can pay $10,000 for his time—the famous chef will work his magic in the customer's own kitchen. Puck seems to relish these events. "The best time was when a prominent wine collector in Chicago flew me to cook for his friends but didn't tell them it was me," Puck told a reporter. "The guests nibbled on hors d'oeuvres, commented on how great the appetizer was, and

DREAMS FOR AFRICA

Like her husband, Gelila Assefa Puck is deeply involved in humanitarian causes. She is a longtime supporter of women's health initiatives and an advocate for African children orphaned by war and AIDS.

In 2010 Assefa Puck established the Dream for Future Africa Foundation. Its mission is to foster opportunities for the continent's most disadvantaged. One of the foundation's major projects is the Gelila Assefa Puck Vocational Center. Located in Aleltu—an Ethiopian village about 55 miles from the national capital, Addis Ababa, where Assefa Puck grew up—the center educates rural children and youth for a variety of careers. "I have never forgotten my Ethiopia where I was born," Assefa Puck said. "I am delighted that we are now seeing tangible results of a dream I have had for years to provide vocational training and life-lasting skills to Ethiopian children who are most at risk."

then the host brought me out to introduce the main course. The look on everyone's face was total shock. It was really fun."

Another highlight was a January 2011 birthday party in Washington, D.C. The guest of honor and her husband loved Asian cuisine, so Puck cooked steamed dumplings; black bass with ginger, garlic, and scallions; and Peking duck. Then Puck brought out a chocolate cake, and President Barack Obama and fifty guests sang "Happy Birthday" to First Lady Michelle Obama.

A month later, Puck was in Los Angeles for the music industry's biggest night. For the fourth straight year, the long-time caterer of the Academy Awards' Governors Ball was also in charge of food for the Grammy Awards celebration. Puck treated the recording artists to dishes such as kung pao organic chicken wings with crushed peanuts and scallions, white-truffle macaroni and cheese, and Kobe beef meatloaf. "The Grammys are all about having fun and letting loose," Puck said. "We play music in the kitchen and everyone is excited. My favorites are classic rock, like Led Zeppelin, The Doors, Pink Floyd, U2 and David Bowie. Classic rock will never go out of style. But I also love playing some Lady Gaga or Jay-Z, to keep things interesting." Puck also said he loved talking with the singers and musicians at the Grammy celebration, many of whom are very knowledgeable about food and wine.

DOING GOOD AND DOING WELL

"I always tell people," Wolfgang Puck once confessed, "it is easier to give than to get for me. There is a lot of joy and happiness if we can give to people."

Puck has been quite generous in giving his money, time, and talent to a wide range of philanthropic causes. A few of the more prominent are the Children's Diabetes Foundation,

Wolfgang poses with Sister Alice Marie Quinn of the St. Vincent Meals on Wheels program in Los Angeles. In October 2011, Puck held a new fundraiser for the organization: a Sunday brunch and charity auction. The mission of St. Vincent Meals on Wheels is to prepare and deliver nutritious meals to homebound seniors and other vulnerable residents across Los Angeles.

the Make-A-Wish Foundation, the Alzheimer's Foundation, and the Lance Armstrong Foundation. Puck cohosts the annual California Spirit Event, a fund-raiser for the American Cancer Society of California. He is a perennial contributor to the Keep Memory Alive event, a benefit for the Cleveland Clinic Lou Ruvo Center for Brain Health in

Las Vegas, which treats neurocognitive disorders such as Alzheimer's disease, multiple sclerosis, and Parkinson's disease. In 2011 the benefit was held the day before the Academy Awards Governors Ball. Still, Puck flew to Las Vegas to join three other chefs in cooking the food for the Keep Memory Alive event before hustling back to Los Angeles for Hollywood's big night. "Chefs are caring, nurturing people," Puck remarked. "Many of us couldn't even imagine not being involved in these causes."

Another cause that Puck feels passionately about is promoting a healthy, sustainable lifestyle. He launched an initiative called WELL (Wolfgang's Eat, Love, Live) to do just that. WELL commits all of Puck's food businesses to using more all-natural, organic, and (where possible) locally produced ingredients. All meat and poultry served must come from farms that meet high standards for the humane treatment of animals, and Puck has expanded the vegetarian selections in all of his restaurants, even the CUT steakhouses. The catering division offers event options with minimal environmental impact.

Puck believes that making responsible decisions about how we eat doesn't require sacrificing the enjoyment of food. "People need to get better food that is really a source of life, which will make their lives better and will taste better and is

In 2011, Wolfgang Puck resigned from the organization that put on the annual American Wine & Food Festival in Los Angeles. During the 28 years that the festival was held (1982–2010), it raised more than $13 million for the Meals-on-Wheels programs of Los Angeles.

more enjoyable," he says. "How can somebody be against that? I truly believe that eating right will help us to live longer and better lives."

Recognizing the toll that not eating right has had on American kids, Puck answered a call from the school board of Nevada's Clark County (which includes the city of Las Vegas). He worked with the Clark County schools' central kitchen to develop healthier fare that students would still want to eat, such as garden-fresh pizza and baked chicken fingers. "We're going to try and move them away from corn dogs and fried foods," Puck said.

ALWAYS LOOKING AHEAD

When the twenty-four-year-old Wolfgang Puck arrived in America in 1973, his goal was to become a top-notch chef and

TREATING ANIMALS HUMANELY

The WELL initiative made sweeping changes in the way Wolfgang Puck's food enterprises do business. Much of WELL focuses on the humane treatment of animals. Working with the Humane Society of the United States, Puck developed a nine-point program. It includes not using any eggs, poultry, pork, or veal from animals raised in cages or crates that prevent them from moving naturally. Puck also stopped serving a longtime staple of French cuisine: foie gras, made from the fatted liver of a force-fed goose or duck.

"We feel the quality of food is better," Puck said of his organization's commitment to more ethical treatment of animals, "and our conscience feels better."

Wolfgang's continuing appearances on Food Network shows, such as Iron Chef and Food Network Star, help him to maintain his status as one of America's most famous chefs.

to have his own restaurant. Obviously, he has accomplished quite a bit more. As a chef, a restaurateur, and an entrepreneur, Puck changed the culinary landscape of his adopted country—several times. And if past is prologue, he'll likely blaze another trail or two for others in the food business to follow.

After decades at the pinnacle of his profession, Puck refuses to be satisfied. "For me," he says, "the past is not important. . . . At the end of the day there is what is today and what is tomorrow."

CHAPTER NOTES

p. 11: "The only thing I told them . . ." April Lisante, "Chefs to the Stars: Wolfgang Puck Talks About Feeding the Oscar Crowd," *Philadelphia Daily News* (February 22, 2007).

p. 12: "The celebrities who come . . . " "VIDEO: Wolfgang Puck Shares his Oscar Dinner Secrets—and Recipes," *People* (March 4, 2010). www.people.com/people/article/0,,20348510,00.html

p. 12: "Don't look for Oscar night . . ." Bill Higgins, "With a Little Bit of Puck," *Variety* (March 4–10, 2002), p. 52.

p. 15: "I taste and taste and . . ." "The Lord of the Onion Rings?; Not When Wolfgang Puck Is in Charge of the Post-Awards Celebrity Feast. But You Can Get the Gold-Dusted Chocolate Oscars," *Hamilton Spectator* (February 27, 2004), p. G06.

p. 17: "His mother is an exquisite cook . . . " Richard Martin, "Wolfgang Puck: Chef, Restaurateur, Celebrity, Los Angeles," *Nation's Restaurant News* (January 1995), p. 160.

p. 18: "I have loved food . . ." Wolfgang Puck, *Wolfgang Puck: Adventures in the Kitchen* (New York: Random House, 1991), p. xv.

p. 18: "I'm still in awe . . ." Martin, "Chef, Restaurateur, Celebrity," p. 160.

p. 19: "Dessert has always been . . ." Sherry Yard, *Desserts by the Yard* (New York: Houghton Mifflin, 2007), p. ix.

p. 20: "I never had fun . . . " Kate Sekules, "Wolfgang Puck, Austria," in *Star Chefs on the Road* (New York: American Express Publishing Corporation, 2005), p. 144.

p. 20: "He wanted me to fight . . ." Nadine Brozan, "Chronicle," *New York Times* (February 19, 1993). http://www.nytimes.com/1993/02/19/style/chronicle-049893.html

p. 20: "Our father worked the mines. . . ." Sekules, *Star Chefs on the Road,* p. 146.

p. 20: "My father told me . . ." Paul Willis, "Wolfgang Puck: Whetting Hollywood's Appetite," CNN.com (August 5, 2009). http://edition.cnn.com/2009/TRAVEL/08/05/wolfgang.puck.bio/

p. 21: "I was so inept . . ." Elizabeth A. Schick, ed., *Current Biography Yearbook 1998* (New York: The H. W. Wilson Company: 1998), p. 479.

p. 22: "If I have to go home . . ." Jesse Katz, "Wolfgang Puck's Home Cooking," *Food & Wine* (August 2007). http://www.foodandwine.com/articles/wolfgang-pucks-home-cooking

p. 24: "was like watching . . . " Marie Speed, "Fresh Approach," *Success* (June 2009), p. 55.

p. 25: "Our dream was to make . . ." "Wolfgang Puck: A Recipe for Success," *A&E Biography*. (A&E Television Networks: 2000).

p. 25: "They put you wherever . . ." M. Barrier, "The Chef as Famous as His Customers," *Nation's Business* (July 1991), p. 29.

p. 28: "It was as if everyone . . ." Sally Howard, "Star Grazing," *Voyager* (May 5, 2011). www.bmivoyager.com/2011/05/01/star-grazing

p. 28: "You wrote it . . ." Liz Welch, "Wolfgang Puck: From Potato Peeler to Gourmet Pizza Tycoon," *INC* (October 2009), p. 87.

p. 30: "If someone dropped a bomb . . ." "In Hollywood, Ma Maison Is 'My House' for the Biggest Stars," *People* (October 31, 1977). http://www.people.com/people/archive/article/0,,20069426,00.html

p. 30: "To be hot . . ." *Current Biography Yearbook 1998*, p. 479.

p. 32: "Together Wolfgang and I . . ." Varsha Mahtani, "Wolfgang Puck," *Nation's Restaurant News* (January 2000), p. 152.

p. 35: "No, this is my . . ." Juliette Rossant, *Super Chef: The Making of the Great Modern Restaurant Empires* (New York: Free Press, 2004), p. 11.

p. 37: "I wanted a bistro . . ." Florence Fabricant, "Chefs Come and Chefs Go, but for Puck, the Flavor Lingers," *New York Times* (July 17, 1991), p. C2.

p. 37: "It was a huge PR stunt . . . " Rossant, *Super Chef*, p. 13.

p. 38: "We just opened . . ." Ibid., p. 12.

p. 39: "The time was right . . . " *Current Biography Yearbook 1998*, p. 479.

p. 39: "My philosophy was influenced . . ." Wolfgang Puck, *Wolfgang Puck's Pizza, Pasta, and More!* (New York: Random House, 2000), pp. xv–xvi.

p. 41: "Although we think of Italy . . ." Wolfgang Puck, *Wolfgang Puck Makes it Easy* (Nashville: Rutledge Hill Press, 2004), p. 100.

p. 41: "pizzas were prisoners . . ." Wolfgang Puck, *Adventures in the Kitchen* (New York: Random House: 1991), p. 176.

p. 43: "He was the first to come . . ." Pamela Parseghian, "Wolfgang Puck," *Nation's Restaurant News* (May 21, 2007), p. 148.

p. 43: "Men have to be . . ." Sekules, *Star Chefs on the Road*, p. 146.

p. 46: "We were besieged . . ." Fabricant, "Chefs Come and Chefs Go," p. C2.

p. 46: "It was very expensive . . ." Rossant, *Super Chef*, p. 15.

p. 47: "We're not French . . . ." Andrea Chang, "How I Made It: Wolfgang Puck, Strong-Willed Chef," *Los Angeles Times* (March 7, 2010). http://www.latimes.com/business/la-fi-himi-puck7-2010mar07,0,7642608,print.story.

p. 48: "I think the most important thing . . ." Brad A. Johnson, "Wolfgang Puck," *Restaurants & Institutions* (August 15, 1995), p. 68.

p. 48: "Barbara makes it happen . . ." "Wolfgang Puck and Barbara Lazaroff Have Cooked Up a Marriage," *People* (March 26, 1984). http://www.people.com/people/archive/article/0,,20087442,00.html

p. 48: "The most important thing is . . ." Robin Lee Allen, " 'Legend' Puck, Industry Pioneers Join Fine Dining Hall of Fame," *Nation's Restaurant News* (June 11, 2007), p. 39.

p. 49: "Johnny would take home . . ." Diane Brady, "Wolfgang Puck," *Bloomberg Businessweek* (January 1, 2011), p. 88.

p. 51: "Joffe created a marketing plan . . ." Rossant, *Super Chef*, p. 26.

p. 51: "The idea was a little bit . . ." Ibid., p. 19.

p. 53: "If I ever have to just attend . . ." Barrier, "The Chef as Famous as His Customers," p. 31.

p. 54: "Joffe envisioned Puck as . . ." Arthur Lubow, "Puck's Peak," *New Yorker* (December 1, 1997), p. 46.

p. 54: "The location is right by the ocean . . ." Fabricant, "Chefs Come and Go," p. C2.

p. 54: "You could have a Friday night . . ." Rossant, *Super Chef*, p. 21.

p. 56: "I kept telling Sheldon . . ." Patricia Martin, "Redefining Dining," *Las Vegas Business Press* (January 1, 1998), p. 3.

p. 56:   "For people who had a flair . . ." Ibid.

p. 58:   "catalyst for the culinary whirlwind . . ." Lisa Jennings, "Wolfgang Puck Fine Dining Group: With an Expanding Catering Division and a Well-known Fine-Dining Brand, the Celebrity Chef Capitalizes on Opportunities to Add to His Culinary Empire," *Nation's Restaurant News* (January 30, 2006), p. 182.

p. 58:   "He's not afraid to be a leader. . . . " Richard Martin, "Wolfgang Puck," p. 160.

p. 58:   "Puck's ability to grow . . ." Steve Coomes, "Hall of Fame: Wolfgang Puck," *Nation's Restaurant News* (May 4, 2009), p. 62.

p. 59:   "A number of years ago . . ." Mahtani "Wolfgang Puck," p. 152.

p. 61:   "My field extends from the kitchen . . ." Rossant, *Super Chef*, p. 35.

p. 62:   "Merchandising is where . . ." Welch, "From Potato Peeler to Tycoon," p. 88.

p. 63:   "We approach the catering . . ." Suzie Amer, "Add a Dash of Fame," *Successful Meetings* (May 2006), p. 37.

p. 64:   "Listen, perhaps this should be . . ." Johnson, "Wolfgang Puck," p. 65.

p. 65:   "Every year we seek out . . ." "NRN Names Puck, Lazaroff 1997 Innovator of the Year Recipients," *Nation's Restaurant News* (June 2, 1997), p. 1.

p. 66:   "What he did in the '80s . . ." Coomes, "Hall of Fame: Wolfgang Puck," p. 62.

p. 67:   "I always go to the newer . . ." Mahtani, "Wolfgang Puck," p. 150.

p. 69:   "I changed back into . . ." Puck, *Wolfgang Puck's Pizza, Pasta and More!*, p. xvi.

p. 70:   "ObaChine is obscene! . . ." Nita Lelyveld, "In Seattle, Logo Eating Them Up: A 1920s Poster in a Restaurant Is Angering Asian Americans," *Philadelphia Inquirer* (April 5, 1998). http://articles.philly.com/1998-04-05/news/25764341_1_seattle-branch-asian-american-asian-immigrants

p. 70:   "I'm a lifelong Seattlite . . ." Ibid.

p. 73:   "If we are all sitting . . ." Kathie Jenkins, "Wolfgang Puck Believes Good Food Should Be Stimulating and Comforting," *Saint Paul Pioneer Press* (January 8, 2001).

p. 74: "He's a very gentle person . . ." Theresa Howard, "Wolfgang Puck," *Nation's Restaurant News* (February 1996), p. 124.

p. 75: "He stands at his station . . . " Mahtani, "Wolfgang Puck," p. 150.

p. 78: "The most difficult thing . . ." Speed, "Fresh Approach," p. 57.

p. 78: "The airlines are a great way . . ." Scott Simon, "Interview: Chef Wolfgang Puck Discusses Airline Food Options," NPR *Weekend Edition Saturday* (January 18, 2003).

p. 78: "We feel that the Wolfgang Puck menu . . ." "Wolfgang Puck Express," *Nation's Restaurant News* (January 31, 2005), p. 204.

p. 82: "People want to be . . ." John Berman, "Overcooked," *Nightline*, March 31, 2009.

p. 83: "It's difficult to find . . ." Howard, "Star Grazing."

p. 83: "I make my team . . ." Ibid.

p. 85: "I am the happiest woman . . ." Jenny Hontz, "A Fashionable Life: Gelila Assefa & Wolfgang Puck," *Harper's Bazaar* (July 2007), p. 71.

p. 85: "We all have this energy . . ." Ibid.

p. 87: "It's the lab. . ." Jennings, "Wolfgang Puck Fine Dining Group," p. 182.

p. 88: "I still believe I got . . ." Allen, "'Legend' Puck," p. 39.

p. 88: "It was beyond . . ." CNN (September 4, 2009). www.cnn.com/video/data/2.0/video/international/2009/09/04/av.3.gelila.puck.cnn.html.

p. 88: "Having grown a little bit older . . ." Patricia Sheridan, "Patricia Sheridan's Breakfast with . . . Wolfgang Puck," *Pittsburgh Post-Gazette* (December 14, 2009). http://www.post-gazette.com/pg/09348/1020713-129.stm

p. 89: "Could you imagine . . ." Maureen Farrell, "Married Celebrity Entrepreneurs," *Forbes* (June 3, 2009). http://www.forbes.com/2009/06/02/married-celebrity-entre-preneurs-entrepreneurs-sales-marketing-married.html

p. 90: "The best time . . ." Tara Weingarten, "A Star in My Kitchen," *Newsweek* (March, 16, 2009), p. 53.

p. 90: "I have never forgotten . . ." "Designer Gelila Assefa Puck and Superchef Wolfgang Puck Report Progress in Philanthropy Work in Ethiopia," Dream for Future Africa. www.dffaf.org/news.html

p. 91: "The Grammys are all about . . ." Wolfgang Puck, "Guest

Blog: Wolfgang Puck Talks Grammys Menu, Rocks Out to Lady Gaga," Zagat.com (February 10, 2011). http://www.zagat.com/buzz/guest-blog-wolfgang-puck-talks-grammys-menu-rocks-out-to-lady-gaga

p. 91: "I always tell people . . ." Speed, "Fresh Approach," p. 57.

p. 92: "Chefs are caring, nurturing . . ." "Serving the Community," *Nation's Restaurant News* (March 10, 2008), p. 41.

p. 92: "People need to get better food . . ." "Wolfgang Puck: Living, Loving, Eating," *Organic Connections* (March 2011), p. 11.

p. 94: "We're going to try. . ." "Serving the Community," p. 42.

p. 94: "We feel the quality of food . . ." Associated Press, "Celebrity Chef Wolfgang Puck Bans Foie Gras, Caged Chickens from New Animal-Friendly Menu," *Reading Eagle* (March 22, 2007). http://readingeagle.com/article.aspx?id=24341

p. 95: "For me, the past . . ." Rossant, *Super Chef*, p. 47–48.

CHRONOLOGY

1949: Wolfgang Puck is born Wolfgang Johannes Topfschnig in St. Veit, Austria, on July 8.

1963: Gets his first position in the restaurant business, as a chef's apprentice at the Hotel Post in Villach, Austria, but is soon fired for ineptitude.

1969: Begins an apprenticeship at L'Oustau de Baumanière, a renowned restaurant in Les Baux, France, operated by the legendary chef Raymond Thuilier.

1973: Immigrates to the United States with his friend Guy LeRoy, living briefly in New York City before moving to Indianapolis.

1975: Puck and LeRoy go to California. Puck becomes head chef at Ma Maison in Los Angeles.

1976: Marries Marie France Trouillot.

1979: Divorces Trouillot.

1981: Puck's first cookbook, *Wolfgang Puck's Modern French Cooking for the American Kitchen*, is published.

1982: In January, Puck and his girlfriend, Barbara Lazaroff, open Spago in West Hollywood. It is an immediate success.

1983: Chinois opens in Santa Monica. Puck and Lazaroff marry.

1986: Puck begins doing regular cooking spots on ABC's *Good Morning America*.

1989: Postrio opens in San Francisco. Puck and Lazaroff's first son, Cameron, is born.

1991: Puck receives his first award from the James Beard Foundation for Outstanding Chef. The first Wolfgang Puck Express opens in San Francisco.

1993: Spago in West Hollywood is inducted into the Nation's Restaurant News Fine Dining Hall of Fame. The first Wolfgang Puck Café opens in Universal City.

1994: Puck and Lazaroff's second son, Byron, is born.

1995: Puck caters the Academy Awards' Governors Ball for the first time. He also begins selling his own line of kitchenware.

1998: Puck receives his second Outstanding Chef of the Year Award from the James Beard Foundation.

1999: Puck becomes an American citizen. He becomes the first chef to appear on *Forbes* magazine's Celebrity 100 list.

2000: *Wolfgang Puck* premieres on the Food Network.

2002: Puck's Food Network show receives a Daytime Emmy for Outstanding Service Show. Puck and Lazaroff divorce.

2005: Puck's fiancée, Gelila Assefa, gives birth to a son, Oliver.

2006: Assefa and Puck's second son, Alexander, is born.

2007: Puck and Assefa marry.

2008: The Culinary Institute of America honors Puck with its Chef of the Year award.

2011: Puck cooks for First Lady Michelle Obama's birthday party, his seventeenth consecutive Academy Awards' Governors Ball, and his fourth consecutive Grammy Awards celebration.

GLOSSARY

BISTRO—a small, unpretentious restaurant.

CALIFORNIA CUISINE—a style of cooking, popularized largely by Wolfgang Puck in the 1970s and 1980s, that stresses the use of fresh, locally harvested ingredients.

CULINARY—having to do with cooking and the kitchen.

EN CROUTE—food that is wrapped in a pastry and baked.

HARICOT VERT—a French green bean, usually longer and thinner than American string beans.

HORS D'OEUVRES—various savory foods served as appetizers.

PAELLA—a traditional Spanish dish consisting of cooked rice, meat or seafood, beans, and other vegetables, often flavored with saffron.

POT STICKER—a crescent-shaped dumpling, filled with meat or vegetables, that is steamed and then fried.

SASHIMI—a traditional Japanese dish consisting of thinly sliced raw fish.

TARTARE—raw meat or fish served with seasonings or sauces.

TEMPURA—seafood or vegetables dipped in batter and deep fried.

TRATTORIA—a usually small Italian restaurant.

FURTHER READING

Food & Wine Magazine. *Star Chefs on the Road: 10 Culinary Masters Share Stories and Recipes.* New York: American Express Food & Wine Magazine Corporation, 2005.

Puck, Wolfgang. *Wolfgang Puck Cookbook: Recipes from Spago, Chinois, and Points East and West.* New York: Random House, 1996.

————. *Wolfgang Puck's Pasta, Pizza, and More!* New York: Random House, 2000.

————. *Live, Love, Eat! The Best of Wolfgang Puck.* New York: Random House: 2002.

————. *Wolfgang Puck Makes It Easy: Delicious Recipes for Your Home Kitchen.* Nashville: Rutledge Hill Press, 2004.

Rossant, Juliette. *Super Chef.* New York: Free Press, 2004.

INTERNET RESOURCES

WWW.WOLFGANGPUCK.COM

> Puck's official website includes a biography, press releases, restaurant locations, recipes, and more.

WWW.FOODNETWORK.COM/RECIPES-AND-COOKING/

WOLFGANG-PUCK/INDEX.HTML

> The Food Network's page for Wolfgang Puck.

WWW.BIOGRAPHY.COM/PEOPLE/WOLFGANG-PUCK-

9542381

> The companion website for the A&E Biography profile of Wolfgang Puck.

HTTP://BARBARALAZAROFF.COM/PHILANTHROPY.PHP

> The official website of Barbara Lazaroff includes information about the American Wine & Food Festival, which Wolfgang Puck co-founded.

WWW.FOODNETWORK.COM/RECIPES-AND-COOKING/

WOLFGANG-PUCK/INDEX.HTML

> Wolfgang Puck's page on the Food Network's website include a biography of the famous chef. The site can also be searched for some of his recipes, as well as videos of Puck in the kitchen.

Numbers in **bold italics** refer to captions.

CONTRIBUTORS

ALISON HART is the author of more than twenty children's books. Her newest titles are *Emma's River* (Peachtree Publishers); *Whirlwind* (Random House), the sequel to her Edgar-nominated *Shadow Horse*; and *Taking the Reins* (American Girls). *Gabriel's Horses*, *Gabriel's Triumph*, and *Gabriel's Journey* (Peachtree) were chosen as Junior Library Guild Premier Selections. The author holds a BS degree in special education/elementary education from the University of Maryland and an MS in communicative disorders from Johns Hopkins University. She is an adjunct instructor of developmental reading and writing at Blue Ridge Community College in Virginia.

Photo credits: Associated Press: 41; © 2007, Food Network: 74; Getty Images: 6, 13, 29, 34, 36, 50, 57, 63, 76; Getty Images for DCP: 92; Joe Skipper/Reuters /Landov: 68; photo by Alan Light: 45; courtesy L'Oustau de Baumanière: 24; NBC/Photofest: 73; used under license from Shutterstock.com: 1, 3, 17, 22, 40, 42; Rudy Balasko / Shutterstock.com: 26; Kushch Dmitry / Shutterstock.com: 47; egd / Shutterstock.com: 10; Helga Esteb / Shutterstock.com: 82 (center, right); Featureflash/Shutterstock.com: 14, 80, 102; Anita Huszti / Shutterstock.com: 19; RoidRanger / Shutterstock.com: 82 (left); Steve Rosset / Shutterstock.com: 52; Max Topchii / Shutterstock.com: 21; © 2011, Television Food Network, G.P.: 95; WireImage: 53, 60, 84; courtesy Wolfgang Puck: 79, 87.

Cover images: © 2007, Food Network (portrait); used under license from Shutterstock.com (collage).